THE WORD FOR THIS CENTURY

THE WORD

FOR THIS CENTURY

CARL F. H. HENRY

KENNETH S. KANTZER

STUART C. HACKETT

T. LEONARD LEWIS

BILLY GRAHAM

GLENN W. BARKER

V. RAYMOND EDMAN

JOHN F. WALVOORD

EDITED BY MERRILL C. TENNEY

Dean of the Graduate School of Wheaton College

 NEW YORK OXFORD UNIVERSITY PRESS 1960

TO FACULTY AND STUDENTS OF THE CENTURY PAST

WHO BY DEVOTED LABOR

"FOR CHRIST AND HIS KINGDOM"

HAVE TAUGHT AND EXEMPLIFIED

THE WORD OF GOD

FOR THEIR GENERATION

AND OURS

THE STATEMENT OF FAITH

Adopted by the Trustees of Wheaton College, March 3, 1926

1. We believe in the Scriptures of the Old and the New Testaments as verbally inspired by God and inerrant in the original writing, and that they are of supreme and final authority in faith and life.

2. We believe in one God, eternally existing in three persons: Father, Son, and Holy Spirit.

3. We believe that Jesus Christ was begotten by the Holy Spirit, born of the Virgin Mary, and is true God and true man.

4. We believe that man was created in the image of God; that he sinned, and thereby incurred, not only physical death, but also that spiritual death which is separation from God; and that all human beings are born with a sinful nature, and, in the case of those who reach moral responsibility, become sinners in thought, word, and deed.

5. We believe that the Lord Jesus Christ died for our sins, according to the Scriptures, as a representative and substitutionary sacrifice; and that all who believe in Him are justified on the ground of His shed blood.

6. We believe in the resurrection of the crucified body of our Lord, in His ascension into Heaven, and in His present life there for us, as High Priest and Advocate.

7. We believe in "that blessed hope," the personal, premillennial, and imminent return of our Lord and Saviour, Jesus Christ.

8. We believe that all who receive by faith the Lord Jesus Christ are born again of the Holy Spirit, and thereby become children of God.

9. We believe in the bodily resurrection of the just and the unjust, the everlasting blessedness of the saved, and the everlasting punishment of the lost.

PREFACE

Etched against the sky of a quiet Midwestern city, the tower of Wheaton College stands sentinel over the campus. For one hundred years Wheaton College has been a landmark of faith to its students who have chosen it as their Alma Mater, and to their parents and friends who have supported its ideals of Christian education.

Under the leadership of four presidents, Jonathan Blanchard (1860–82), his son Charles Albert Blanchard (1882–1925), J. Oliver Buswell, Jr. (1926–40), and V. Raymond Edman (1940–   ), Wheaton has maintained a consistent witness to Christian truth. Through numerous economic depressions, three major wars, and the shifting scenes of social and theological controversy, it has stood firmly for an undiluted Christian faith. Its faculty and graduates have been champions of political liberty, social reform, and evangelistic fervor.

In 1937 the Graduate School of Theology was established as the result of a generous provision in the form of a residuary trust from the estate of John Dickey, Jr., of Philadelphia, in order that Wheaton's ministry might be enlarged. Since the inception of the Graduate School more than three hundred and fifty alumni have been graduated and have entered the ranks of teaching, the ministry, and the mission field.

This volume is issued on the centennial anniversary of Wheaton College as a testimony to its historic faith. The contributors of these essays, representing administration, faculty, and alumni, are actively engaged in preaching and teaching this message, and they speak for the larger number seeking to present the word of God to this century.

As the list of authors on the title page of this book indicates, it is the product of co-operative effort by men whose time is heavily taxed by the daily duties in which they are engaged. To them the Graduate School of Wheaton College is indebted for their contribution to this memorial volume. One of them, Dr. T. Leonard Lewis, the President of Gordon College, was suddenly taken home to be with the Lord in the spring of this year, and the chapter that he wrote is one of the last products of his pen. To all of these men hearty thanks are due for their willing participation.

Special thanks are offered to Dr. Carl F. H. Henry and to his publisher, Wm. B. Eerdmans Publishing Company, for permission to quote two paragraphs from his *Christian Personal Ethics*.

The Centennial Committee of Wheaton College, Richard Gerig, Chairman, has aided materially in sponsoring this project. The Editor acknowledges gratefully the help of his wife, Helen J. Tenney, in preparing the manuscript for publication, and the stenographic work of Mrs. Edward A. Adams in the transcription of the copy.

Merrill C. Tenney

Wheaton, Illinois
November 1959

CONTENTS

CONTENTS

INTRODUCTION

MERRILL C. TENNEY

Merrill C. Tenney is Dean of the Graduate School of Wheaton College and J. P. Williston Professor of Bible and Theology. He received his training at Gordon College (Th.B.), Boston University (A.M.), and Harvard University (Ph.D.). He taught New Testament at Gordon College from 1930 to 1943, and at Wheaton from 1943 to the present time. He has served as Dean of the Graduate School since 1947. Among his publications are John: The Gospel of Belief *(1948),* Galatians: The Charter of Christian Liberty *(1950),* The New Testament: A Survey *(1953), and* Interpreting Revelation *(1957).*

During the last hundred years greater changes have taken place within the life and thought of our world than occurred in the preceding half millennium. Measured in terms of the transformation of life within the United States, the era following the outbreak of the Civil War has produced an entirely new outlook on our culture. The abolition of slavery and the ascendancy of federal union over states' rights, the settlement of the West and the closing of the frontier, the increase in immigration and the growth of public education, have made the citizens of America a different race from those who determined its destinies a century ago. Now, after participation in two world wars, the American influence is global, and "the American way of life" is recognized everywhere as a distinct philosophy of existence, whether it is liked or not.

Political and social changes have been accompanied by religious changes as well. America is still an eminently Protestant country, though Roman Catholicism commands the allegiance of a slowly increasing group of people. Judaism is a minority, but is both vocal and powerful. Many who are classed as Protestant are really noncommittal; they are labeled as Protestant because they cannot be called anything else. A vast number have no clear convictions on religious matters; they are confused or indifferent, or both.

Such confusion and indifference does not bode well for the national future. Every nation that has ever risen to power has done so on the basis of some religious or political conviction, behind which were certain postulates for which men would gladly live and die. The founding fathers of this country may not all have been religious men or Christian men; but the majority of them maintained that freedom was man's right as a being created by God, and that he should claim and defend that freedom under the law that sprang from a concept of divine justice. Loss of this conviction may well bring ultimate loss of the freedom which we cherish.

Two concepts of freedom are contending for domination of the world today. Communism contends that freedom lies in the uniformity of the mass man. Without the profit motive, which can lead to poverty on the part of the laborer and to wealth on the part of the employer, the classless society will be introduced in which all will prosper equally without oppression. In order to introduce this society, however, the state must ruthlessly abolish all of the old standards, and even destroy religion, which recognizes the authority and rulership of God. Man thus becomes his own standard and savior. Material welfare becomes the supreme good. Expediency rather than truth is the rule of life. The present is the complete scope of man's existence; eternity is illusory.

Although the full consequences of the communist philosophy are not accepted by all, its prevailing materialism and practical atheism have become more widespread than its economic system. Many people who would indignantly repudiate the suggestion that they are "Red" or even "pink" are essentially as materialistic and as atheistic as the most radical communist. The peril of this century is that while we may not succumb to the brainwashing tactics of official Communism, the infiltration of its anti-Christian spirit may very easily undermine the foundations of the faith and culture that we inherit.

The only answer to such materialism and atheism is the gospel; but what constitutes the gospel? Again we are confronted by tremendous changes in theological thought. The liberalism of the past half-century affirmed that the gospel was the fatherhood of God, the brotherhood of man, salvation by character, and the gradual but inevitable improvement of the world by the amelioration of social wrongs. Man was daily becoming better and better, and would ultimately outgrow the vestiges of his crude and brutal past. The holocaust of two world wars dispelled this illusion; and the dreams of self-betterment vanished in the gas chambers of Dachau and in the reeking beachheads of Guadalcanal. Today we are staggering under a vast disillusionment. We have discovered that we are not better than our fathers, who, if our boasted progress is true, had more excuse for their cruelties than we have. Is our civilization simply an elegant veneer to cover our aimlessness and our futility?

Neo-orthodoxy has given a partial answer. Man must meet God, it says. He must acknowledge that God is sovereign and gracious; that man is a helpless sinner, and that only in the encounter between the individual who repents and the God who manifests grace can he be saved. Insofar as this system demands a recognition of saving power on God's part and of human sinfulness, it is right; but on what basis does neo-orthodoxy make this demand? Has God spoken unmistakably? Where is the starting point for this theology? Have we a reliable revelation on which we can build? The answer of neo-orthodoxy at this point is not clear and unequivocal. The Scriptures, it says, are a witness to truth, but cannot be taken as final truth. The Bible contains error as well as truth. It is the means through which God speaks to us, but the account may at times be blurred. If it does bring a clear message, it does so as the Holy Spirit makes it the Word of God for us, not because its phrases are intrinsically God's Word.

Such a view leaves a margin of uncertainty in its thinking. Can falsehood be distinguished if it is inextricably intermingled with truth in the same writing? Are we astute enough to know when the Spirit is speaking and when the interpretation is simply the result of subjective preference? Evangelicals contend that the Bible *is* the Word of God, and that its history and teachings are alike the vehicle of God's communication to all generations since it was written. Of course, it must be translated into the language of the current era, and its truths must be applied to modern conditions; but the truths themselves are older than the conditions to which they are to be applied. The Bible may say nothing about airplanes, but its precepts apply as well to men who fly planes as they did to men who drove chariots.

One hundred years ago, on a barren knoll of a Midwestern prairie, a small group of men knelt in prayer. Realizing the need for a Christian educational institution in which their children could be trained for godliness and good citizenship, they committed themselves and their fortunes to this important enterprise. From this humble beginning has grown Wheaton College, an institution which is firmly committed to the permanent relevance of the revelation of God in Christ to the contemporary scene. During the century it has stood uncompromisingly for the evangelical faith and for the highest standards in personal character, in social betterment, and in cultural attainments. Its position is epitomized in the motto carved on the cornerstone of its main building: FOR CHRIST AND HIS KINGDOM.

The eight essays prepared for this book summarize Wheaton's message for the contemporary world. They are based on its statement of faith, and are written by representative members of its administration, faculty, and alumni, under the sponsorship of the Graduate School of Wheaton College. The writers are offering these essays as their contributions to the centenary celebration of the college (1959–60). They speak from the varied viewpoints of the administrator, the scholar, and the evangelist, and they differ in approach and style. Nevertheless they bear united testimony to the core of evangelical faith. God has spoken His final word to men through the historical Christ, and because Christ still lives His truth is applicable to our age.

"The Word for This Century" must be Christ's word. Though it may be understood only partially and mediated imperfectly, it is an acknowledgement of His authority and an expression of positive faith in His adequacy for the dilemma of our day.

THE WORD FOR THIS CENTURY

ONE

MAN'S DILEMMA: SIN

CARL F. H. HENRY

Carl F. H. Henry was graduated from Wheaton College (A.B.) and from the Wheaton Graduate School (A.M.). He received his B.D. and Th.D. degrees from Northern Baptist Theological Seminary, and his Ph.D. from Boston University. He has taught at Northern Baptist Seminary (1940–42), and at Fuller Theological Seminary in the field of Systematic Theology (1946–58) and is currently Editor of Christianity Today. *He is author of numerous books, including* Remaking the Modern Mind *(1946),* The Uneasy Conscience of Modern Fundamentalism *(1947), and* Christian Personal Ethics *(1957).*

The observation that mankind no longer troubles itself about sin is outdated and outworn. The present concern may sometimes seem surface and shallow, but nonetheless it betrays an underlying sense of moral anxiety. "You cannot take all luggage with you on all journeys. . . . Even your right hand and your right eye may be among the things you have to leave behind." So C. S. Lewis, in the preface to *The Great Divorce*, challenged the once popular notion that evil can metamorphose into good. His trenchant words reflect the fresh exploration of our age into the awesome fact of human depravity.

I

Ironically enough, the past century overlaps the proud modern era which at its outset spoke so prophetically of man's earthly glory and now, but not so poignantly, bemoans his predicament. When Charles Darwin's *On the Origin of Species* appeared a hundred years ago, the intellectuals were increasingly more certain of man's animal heritage than of any divine creation. They anticipated a benevolent earthly kingdom spawned by the genius of experimental science rather than a supernatural kingdom of righteousness based upon divine regeneration of sinful men. The generation before World War I disparaged the idea of man's *dilemma* no less than that of his fall and sinfulness, for while remnants of an animal ancestry were affirmed, they were assumed to be fast vanishing. By virtue of the evolutionary process, mankind and society presumably were rising to ever higher potential and achievement. Only surviving strands of selfishness stood between man and his day of earthly bliss. Such traces of a bestial past, however, no longer resided in man's nature and will; they adhered, rather, to the fringe of life, somewhat like a useless tail. Given enough time, perhaps by one more generation, and quite probably by the twentieth century, these retards, likewise, would be fully overcome. Then, freed and independent of such traditional props as supernatural grace and spiritual rebirth, the human species would fully manifest its inherent perfection.

A minor sound, however, began to dull this happy and optimistic hymn to human nature. The pessimism of Sigmund Freud declared that "psychoanalysis . . . confirms what the pious were wont to say, that we are all miserable sinners." Man is veritably riddled with guilt feelings, he said. Hate and aggression are such fixed components of human nature that they cannot be transcended by evolutionary progress. Moreover, even the most balanced individuals are subject to periodic neurosis. Freud viewed man's lapse into neurosis as humanity's "original sin," a psychoanalytic fall that recurs in each individual's recapitulation of the development of the race. His theory of the Oedipus complex, the repressed infantile sexual attachment of the son for his mother, is of only secondary importance to us here, though it is noteworthy, of course, that he applied his exclusively sexual interpretation of life even to the central facts of the Judeo-Christian religion. In *Moses and Monotheism*, for example, Freud explains the "murders" of Moses and Christ as a re-enactment of man's murder of his primeval father. Other Freudian tenets are more serviceable to a study of sin, however. His recognition of the sense of guilt pervading the sex life of fallen man is significant. According to Freud, even normalcy includes a degree of neurosis. For this reason, all men are "miserable sinners." Further, since all men are perennially plagued by a sense of guilt, their consequent struggle with a neurotic character is suggestive of the "second nature" in Biblical theology.

To many observers evolutionary optimism and Freudian pessimism presented rival estimates of man's nature. Both, however, reflected one common spirit. Each shared in the secular revolt against revealed religion and the Biblical view of man. While evangelical forces energetically sought to protect their doctrine from onslaughts of naturalistic evolution and psychoanalysis, they no doubt were more effective in propounding their own views than in unmasking the weakness of the secular alternatives. For one thing, the competing alternatives were not fixed and final; further and naturally enough, Christians were better informed on their own heritage. It became apparent, however, that if the twentieth century was to avert catastrophe, it must be diverted from Darwin and Freud, and restored to Jesus and Paul.

Darwinianism guffawed at the *sense of sin*, while Freudianism made it responsible for man's predicament. The underlying metaphysic of both views, however, excluded any recognition of *sin* itself as an objective reality in the Judeo-Christian sense. The most that Freud acknowledges is a sense of guilt, and on occasion he identifies this merely with the feeling of anxiety. Psychoanalytic studies as well as evolutionary expositions jeopardized particularly the moral status of guilt feelings and their relationship to the supernatural world. The Freudian "fall" is inevitable because of the weakness of human nature; it does not involve a moral decision for which the human ego is responsible. Guilt in the theological sense is therefore eliminated, a maneuver whose consequences are revolutionary. For, as James Orr reminds us in the opening lines of *Sin as a Problem of Today*, "What we name sin is, from the religious point of view, the tragedy of God's universe." Sin is nothing less than man's transgression *against God*, the revolt of the creature's will against the will of the holy Creator. Man's waywardness gains its derogatory character as sin from this fact alone. The departure from this postulate necessarily involved secular theories in a misunderstanding of both the character and magnitude of man's quandary. Eventually the very concept of sin was obliterated.

The Freudian school considers the evil that indwells human nature a permanent, essential, and normal experience. Freud's "fallen men" are neurotics who have "sinned" against the superego. Therapy is sufficient for their healing; the living God is as unnecessary to their restoration or redemption as He is to their fall. Darwinian principles also emphasized the normalcy of sin for this stage of man's development. Obviously the Biblical writers would express the highest disapproval of such declarations. For Biblical theology the fall is neither essential nor normal for human nature as originally and divinely fashioned in the Creator's sacred image. Without a sovereign personal Creator to whom man stands in responsible relationship, man's sense of sin and guilt is devoid of theological content. Sin actually belongs to the sphere of religion and theology, and apart from man's relationship to God, moral evil loses its character as sin. Depriving sin of its supernatural orientation deflates it to mere psychological or sociological flabbiness.

Such failure to accept the theological concept of sin and guilt characterized a wide diversity of contemporary notions of moral evil. Representative of this theological derailment is Bertrand Russell's statement in *Human Society in Ethics and Politics:* " 'Sin,' except in the sense of conduct toward which the agent, or the community, feels an emotion of disapproval, is a mistaken concept, calculated to promote needless cruelty and vindictiveness when it is others that are thought to sin, and a morbid self-abasement when it is ourselves whom we condemn."

In her book *Man as a Sinner in Contemporary American Realistic Theology,* Mary Frances Thelen noted: "Teachers of the philosophy of religion and systematic theology in the major liberal seminaries of the first third of the twentieth century have little in their writings on the subject of sin." Similarly, in surveying the theological situation in America, William Adams Brown in *Beliefs That Matter,* in 1928, singled out "a loss of the sense of sin" as one of the prominent marks of contemporary religion. Clergymen were "preaching about almost everything else except the forgive-

ness of sins." During these lean years of liberalism, the call
of evangelism went begging in the regular churches, and
therefore passed by default to independent and interdenomi-
national enterprises.

It was this development, in fact, which enlarged the ministry of the Christian colleges and Bible institutes. Also it
brought radio voices like that of Charles E. Fuller on "The
Old-Fashioned Revival Hour" to national familiarity. It was
such enterprises that maintained the continuity of evangelical witness in a day when faith suffered from spiritual malaise
in established ecclesiastical centers. Because of secular dis-
regard for the scriptural view, evangelicals became impelled
to indict the non-Christian theories of man and his plight
in history. Wherever evangelical doctrine was proclaimed,
sin therefore continued to represent the serious blemish that
the Law and the Gospel claimed it to be.

To thwart the spiritual decay that inevitably follows lax
views of conscience and disparagement of divine commandments and precepts, evangelical agencies saw the necessity
of proclaiming Christianity as a unitary world-wide view.
They knew that deviations from any of the revealed doctrines, especially from those of sin and redemption, bear
inescapable reactions for the whole orbit of belief and life.
The effects of such distortion permeate the entire range of
Christian doctrine. In the sphere of Christology, sin im-
plicates not simply our Lord's redemptive work, but the very
integrity of His person. To distort the facts about sin yields
a misconception of duty and of the life of virtue that
threatens the very foundation of true Christian ethics.

Evangelical scholars recognized this inseparable connection between the dread facts of human sin, corruption, and
guilt and the Christian tenets of redemption much better
than the mediating thinkers of the day. Christianity makes

the concept of sin unmistakably definite; only this careful delineation gives any significance to the utter indispensability of the new birth, of justification and sanctification, in short, of saving reliance on Jesus Christ.

By stripping away first one component and then another of the Biblical doctrine of sin, modernist theories erased also the notion that man deserved divine wrath, or that any penalty was required. They rejected the doctrine of depravity and softened the delineations of evil. The task of the evangelical leaders therefore involved battling against both the fully secular trends and the mediating currents as well. Although retaining the concept of sin as a violation of divine Law, the mediating school nonetheless abbreviated man's responsibility (in deference to evolutionary modes of thought) to his present capacity to do the good. This limitation absolved him of any penalty for the Adamic fall and its consequences.

Evangelical leaders, of course, were called on to maintain a far more serious exposition of man's predicament. Furthermore, while liberal thinkers rejected the moral relevance of sinless perfection, evangelical teachers upheld God's ideal for man as announced at creation. Warning that man's holy destiny had been violated by the fall, evangelicals insisted on his need for ultimate restoration to absolute purity as basic to an eternal glorious destiny. In the flesh of Jesus of Nazareth they acclaimed the perfect embodiment of divine righteousness. They hailed man's participation in the benefits of that righteousness, through imputation and sanctification, and rejoiced in the ultimate prospect of total conformity to Christ's moral image.

II

Unlike earthquakes and floods which so troubled the philosophers a century ago, the terrors of the twentieth century resulted from moral rather than natural evils. Man's iniquity forced a reappraisal of both secular and religious optimism. The mass slaughter and enslavement of humanity, the scientific creation of increasingly efficient weapons of destruction, and contemporary man's anguished and meaningless existence pointed ever more surely to one humbling admission: humanity is indeed fallen from its divine intention, is estranged from its high destiny, and is enmeshed in the universal and continuing predicament of sin.

That some moderns denied the inevitability of such a far-reaching conclusion is obvious enough. Logical positivists were not alone in denouncing everything but their own presumptuous and naturalistic presuppositions. They heralded themselves as agents of comfort (to the sinner) by ascribing unreality to terms like sin and God and soul. In Britain, men like C. S. Lewis and T. S. Eliot provoked Kathleen Nott's excoriating ridicule and anger over the revival of "the dogma of original sin." In America, even some religious theories continued to take shallow soundings of moral evil. *Evil and the Christian Faith* by Nels Ferré, professor of theology at Andover-Newton Seminary, professes to take sin seriously, yet it avoids the notion of original sin by granting a highly fanciful significance to the Garden of Eden story. Ferré considers sin a necessary stage in man's development, and even places a premium upon it: "Rebellion against God is necessary at some point in our lives if we are to become free sons, glorifying Him out of love and gratitude. . . . Every man, if he is not to remain an animal, if he is to rise to moral decision, revolts against God, hides from Him, questions Him, perhaps even hates Him. . . . Evil is basically due to the necessity of our rebellion, at least in temptation, that we might be free. . . ." Ferré's remark that "modern theology is in danger of taking man the creature and his sin too seriously" is no more surprising than his repugnance and revulsion over the divine punishment of man's sins and the Biblical doctrine of hell. His approach is but one of many speculative analyses of sin to be found in our era. Almost as if to compensate for disallowing the depth of personal involvement in sin, many contemporary writers focus their consciences instead upon social wrongs and vent their righteous indignation against these.

The most blatant assault on the revival of a theology of sin came, curiously enough, from communist sources interested in a collectivistic revision of the social order. They repudiated Christian morality on the basis of a naturalistic world-and-life framework. In their effort to replace God with the totalitarian state they defined the Fall as man's defection from primitive communism. The fall, sin, and salvation thus had a primarily economic meaning. In Mary Frances Thelen's words, "The historic Fall in Marxism was not a perverse moral choice by a representative of mankind but merely greater economic production, which led quite naturally to exchange of surplus goods, and then to specialization and division of labor. . . . The correction of the evil, therefore, is also non-moral, economic, and sociological reform rather than repentance and moral regeneration."

The larger theology of Europe and of the Anglo-Saxon world as a whole, however, has expressed a contrary tendency. Instead of weakening the sense of sin, it has classified sin as the root of man's dilemma. It has reinforced this emphasis because of the recent drift of history and of post-

Freudian studies of human personality as much as from a new appreciation of Biblical psychology. The attempt of F. R. Tennant, formerly lecturer at Cambridge University, in *The Origin and Propagation of Sin* and *The Concept of Sin* to reduce sin to voluntary disobedience of the divine will has incurred R. Newton Flew's sharp criticism. In *The Idea of Perfection in Christian Theology*, Flew emphasizes that "our worst sins are often those in which we are unconscious." More recently Tennant's position was repudiated by Frederic Reeves, principal of Didsbury College in Bristol, formerly one of Tennant's own students.

In *The Meaning of Sin*, Reeves acknowledges that "so great was the impression made upon me, as upon all his students [by Tennant] that it has taken me a quarter of a century to gain courage openly to differ from him." This reversal from equating sin with deliberate personal rebellion prepares the way for recognizing sin in its larger sense of egocentricity, rather than simply sensuality. Reeves properly insists that the widespread failure of psychologists to understand man's guilt as an objective fact (rather than as subjective feeling) impedes the theological understanding of guilt.

Actually, not until the third decade of the twentieth century did the Anglo-Saxon world again see signs of a realistic appraisal of sin as a willful revolt against the sovereign, holy God. Especially influential was Reinhold Niebuhr. His Gifford Lectures on *The Nature and Destiny of Man* grasped the human dilemma not simply as moral but as theological, and ascribed the utopian illusions of liberalism to "the basic error of negating the fact of original sin." The idea of original sin, which liberal theology had dismissed as anachronism, became once more the indispensable category for understanding man's plight. The very title of H. Shelton Smith's book, *Changing Conceptions of Original*

Sin, cautions against hoping for a full return to the Biblical exposition, and against expecting modern ingenuity to allow itself only one method of revision.

The new emphasis on "original sin" by Karl Barth and then Emil Brunner in the second and third decades provoked considerable theological action and reaction in Europe. Similarly in America, Niebuhr's views became a formative core of anthropological debate, and motivated rival expositions. All of them shared, however, a common rejection of the "chronological view" of original sin; that is, they discounted the Biblical assignment of "original sin" to the first man in a past period of pristine perfection "before the Fall." For them the scriptural view had only a "mythical relevance"; while not considered to be literal history, the Biblical account was prized for mirroring a fundamental fact of human experience. Modern thinkers now substitute the "existential view" of the Fall for the "chronological view." They find the locus of original perfection in those moments of everyman's consciousness in which the self transcends itself. Original perfection is no longer equated with an absolute righteousness wholly exempt from the corruptions of sin. While the contemporary view does not consider original sin as necessary, it nonetheless affirms it to be unavoidable and inevitable. Niebuhr locates the Fall in the ongoing history of the human race. Paul Tillich, on the other hand, associates man's plight with that of the cosmic order and asserts a transcendent Fall.

While Niebuhr complains that Tillich's view leads to the "fatefulness of sin," his own critics level this selfsame charge against Niebuhr. The correlation of human responsibility with sin's inevitability in the experience of man as created remains the vulnerable feature of the newer speculations, however much more sober their view of sin may be. For this reason, certain scholars see in this revival of the emphasis on sin a very real danger to morality. No matter how much personal involvement is retained, sin as a "mysterious cosmic disaster," or as a predicament implicit in man's creation, nonetheless endangers human responsibility and introduces artificiality into the moral order. The modern theories fail to provide a convincing link between man's predicament and his moral responsibility.

In fact, to discount the Biblical explanation of man's tragedy shadows Christian revelation itself with instability and uncertainty. Professor Tillich's exposition supplies a pointed illustration of this fact. In the art, literature, and philosophy of our era Tillich rightly detects the meaninglessness of purely horizontal living. But while these communications may indeed mirror man's struggle in an age when life has lost its dimension of depth, are these statements (even Professor Tillich's, if we may say so) adequate formulations of man's dilemma? They may mirror the nausea of man's soul, his usually desolate, vacuous existence, the anxiety that plagues even his isolated high hours, his enslavement by the demonic. But they do not lead us into that dark chamber of horrors where echoes and re-echoes the resonant voice of the inspired writers: "All have sinned and come short of the glory of God"; "without shedding of blood there is no remission." Professor Tillich repudiates the relevance of Judeo-Christian religion in its historic meaning, and grants only a symbolic significance to the fall of man and to the Biblical doctrine of salvation from sin through the Saviour.[1] Such symbolism disintegrates theology in the solvents of psychology.

The modern rationalizations are indeed a commentary on man's predicament of soul, and furnish insight into his continuous dilemma in all ages and places. Only divine revelation, however, suffices to measure the dire depths of that dilemma. Fully exposed to the wrath of a righteous God, finite and fallen man must find rescue in the Lamb of God who only can remove the sin of the world. So dreadful is man's plight that if Christ has not indeed risen from the dead even believing men remain in their sins.

The most disturbing feature of the present theological revival is its refusal to wrestle earnestly with revealed doctrines of Scripture. More critical rather than Biblical in approach, modern thinkers are wont to dismiss the ideal of a consistent theology of scriptural revelation. Few are alert to the necessity of exhibiting man's nature and responsibility in the coherent context of a world-and-life framework. Most do not seek patiently a systematic perspective by examining current expositions of man's predicament in the light of the Bible.

III

This criticism applies in some measure to evangelical no less than to more speculative thinkers. Unfortunately, contemporary Protestant preaching, not only by itinerant evangelists but also by established pastors, often proclaims the realities of sin and redemption in such generalities that the message becomes ambiguous, perhaps even misleading. That by state man is a sinner in thought, word, and deed, is heard often enough. Affirmed, too, is that the Gospel demands not simply the admission and relief of guilt-feelings, but a forthright acknowledgment of guilt. Neglected, however, is exposition of the nature of guilt, corruption, and penalty, and of the ground of man's predicament in the fall of Adam as well as his own rebellion.

In view of this lack, and in keeping with it, the proclamation of salvation is similarly incomplete. Clergymen speak of the need for faith and "commitment to Christ" and for being "born again." Too often they fail to lay bare the doctrine of the atonement — our Lord's substitutionary and propitiatory death for sinners, the imputation of His righteousness to all who repose their trust in Him. Sometimes even the forgiveness of sins is slighted. Men are saved, of course, by accepting the redemptive mercy of God, and not merely by admission of their wicked deeds; but the sinner unsure of or untaught in the character of sin and salvation remains peculiarly susceptible to spiritual trouble.

For that reason it is encouraging to note in some recent literature on sin an earnest grappling with certain neglected phases of the doctrines of sin and of atonement. Discussions on objective guilt and punishment, as well as on original sin, now give promise of greater spiritual insight and stability. An authentic analysis, that is, in terms of Biblical theology, avoids divorcing sin from the great historical realities prominent in revealed religion. This total panorama includes the revelation of moral law to the nature and will of the sovereign, holy Creator; the inner association of the divine commandments with the fundamental principles of love for God and neighbor; the fall of the first human couple; the impact of their sin upon all creation; the involvement of the whole of humanity in their guilt; the corruption of the whole human race; the divine institution of sacrifice; the provision of atonement by the God-man for the sins of mankind. The most virile theology of the times recognizes that only admission of the Biblical emphasis that all, not merely part, of the personality is sinful can properly explain the human predicament. The whole race is sinful; not simply certain individuals. Because man's nature is sinful, sin remains an inevitability of his present condition; he deliberately wills to sin and is therefore personally responsible even in the midst of this inevitability. Thus modern knowledge may reinforce rather than counteract the Biblical emphasis on man's fallen nature and sinful character. Contemporary theories based on evolutionary premises, however, stop short of tracing this predicament to the fall of our first parents from primeval holiness. Neither do they consider the physical and spiritual death of the race as a penal consequence of that primal fall.

Rather, they seek an ethical interpretation of the universality of sin which buttresses the organic unity of the race but avoids the representative headship of Adam. To do this complicates exposition of redemption as well as of the doctrine of sin, for Biblical revelation views Adam's sin as the immediate cause of inborn depravity, guilt, and condemnation to the whole human race. The Bible also suggests a parallel between the representative headship of the First and Second Adams; imputation of the guilt of the one and the righteousness of the other; inheritance of a corrupt nature from the one and of a righteous nature from the other; exposure to penalty through the one and prospect of adoption through the other.

It remains the sober responsibility of evangelical leaders to expound Christian doctrine in this complete sense, and by it to evaluate and not simply to condemn contemporary modifications and denials. In a time of cultural conflict and crisis, evangelical enterprises must practice this kind of positive presentation. Speculative theories still provide no firm basis for moderating the Biblical fact that moral destiny is not a matter of individual determination. Personal responsibility and decision, of course, remain crucial and inescapable. They are linked on the one hand, however, with the past history of the race, especially with the first man and woman. Endowed with the awesome image of God, this pair was qualified for intimate spiritual fellowship.

On the other hand, personal responsibility and decision are related to the redemptive center of human history. By His incarnation and atonement, Jesus Christ rescues those who lodge their trust in Him from the terrible consequences of human rebellion. The parallelism of Scripture clearly sketches the relationship between the doomed sinner and Adam and between the redeemed sinner and Christ. To dismiss pertinent Pauline references as Rabbinic modes of thought constitutes no decisive refutation. Even Rabbinic passages were not in all respects incorrect, being sometimes based on divine revelation. A decisive and crucial issue is their reliability. Modern theories are constructed primarily in deference to speculative ideas of human nature and redemption. These must be critically viewed from the Biblical norm.

Young ministers could profit from surveying the history of thought in this matter, instead of becoming one-sidedly enamored of current notions. In special pursuits in anthropology and soteriology, and in systematic theology, as well, I personally remember the benefits of working through the careful tabulations on the competitive views in A. H. Strong's *Systematic Theology*. Contemporary theology may be impatient with excursions of this kind. The reason for such impatience, however — revolt against the historic Scriptural view that divine revelation is expressed in doctrinal truth — ought to warn alert evangelicals against acceding to these alien views. The contemporary mind is learning that the problem lies not in improving the classic definition of sin as lack of conformity to God's moral law either in act, disposition, or state, nor in the discrimination of selfishness (as opposed to love of God and neighbor) as the root principle of sin. If evangelical theology faithfully fulfills its primary mission of presenting an effective remedy for sin, the prodigal modern spirit may find the way back to the Father's house.

Scrutiny of the evangelical outlook of the past decade reveals shortcomings, particularly in explaining the meaning of sin in the life of the believer (where it should be discerned with greatest depth). The prevalence of regarding Christianity simply as a religion of private devotion has often slighted or minimized the problem of social justice. Such neglect of Christianity as a world and life view is a great misfortune, which has bequeathed an unchallenged opportunity to humanistic and idealistic agencies to promote their own secular theories of the social order. Even the sphere of Christian personal ethics betrays a certain ethical shallowness by a widespread tendency to equate Christian obedience primarily with negative abstinence from certain worldly practices. The neglect of careful moral teaching that unveils spiritual sins as fully as sins of the flesh has yielded an age of unstable conscience. One of the tasks of a revival of Christian ethics will be to lead the churches into deeper sensitivity to sin. Only a spiritual awakening, with a virile awareness of the wickedness of pride aand lovelessness, holds new promise of a holier hour in the history of the Church.

In *Sin as a Problem of Today*, James Orr spoke of sin as "a terrible fact, the reality, seriousness, and universality of which cannot reasonably be gainsaid," and added that "to exaggerate the persistence, the gravity, the depraving and destroying power of this evil thing" is hardly possible. Moreover, it is only the Judeo-Christian religion that pulsates so persistently with a recognition of the fact and dread toll of moral evil. All this would yield only despair were it not that alongside the terrible fact of man's sin Christianity proclaims the glorious prospect of the forgiveness of sins. If the incarnation — Christ's perfect embodiment of the will of God in the flesh — rebukes us all and cancels any lingering uncertainties we may entertain of God's moral intention and requirement, it nonetheless relieves our dismal hopelessness with the assurance that "God sent not His Son into the world to condemn the world; but that the world through Him might be saved" (Jn. 3:17).

The religion of revelation unmasks our proud pretensions, and bares the unrelieved horrors of sin. But it is also a religion of redemption; alongside the drab news of man's sin and guilt, his corruption and exposure to divine wrath, it publishes also the good tidings of salvation. C. Ryder Smith reminds us in *The Bible Doctrine of Sin* that in the New Testament "sin is not only serious, but fatal . . . God's 'love' shows itself, not in the assurance that sin 'does not matter,' but in the offer of salvation from it. It 'matters' so much that it demands the Cross. If the Christian Church is 'obsessed with sin,' as some complain, so is the Christian God."

When asked what he considered his greatest discovery, the great Scottish surgeon, Sir James Simpson, replied: "That I am a sinner and that Jesus Christ is a great Saviour." It is fortunate indeed that fallen man still lives in an hour of decision. In the midst of his sins, he may yet hear the evangelistic summons of the believing Church. He may yet experience the forgiveness of sins, and thereby discover the only means for the avoidance of their penalty, and for their conquest as well. We take heart, therefore, because the light of the Gospel not only clearly reveals man's guilt, but also opens the way to sin's removal.

TWO

THE AUTHORITY OF THE BIBLE

KENNETH S. KANTZER

*Kenneth S. Kantzer is Charles Deal Professor of Theology
and Chairman of the Division of Biblical Education and
Apologetics in Wheaton College. He is a graduate of
Ashland College (A.B.), Ohio State University (A.M.),
Faith Theological Seminary (B.D., S.T.M.), and Harvard
Divinity School (Ph.D.). He has served in Wheaton Col-
lege and Graduate School since 1946.*

In a famous essay on revelation Archbishop William
Temple strikes the keynote for theological thinking in our
day. He writes, "The dominant problem of contemporary
religious thought is the problem of revelation. Is there such
a thing at all? If there is, what is its mode and form? Is it
discoverable in all existing things or only in some? If in
some, then in which? And by what principles are these
selected as its vehicle? Where is it found? Or believed to be
found? What is its authority?" [1]

This contemporary debate about revelation is no tempest
in a teapot. It reflects two things. First it attests once again
that the topic "revelation" is of fundamental significance for
human existence. Long before Christians carried the gospel

to the ancient world, men agonized over questions about
the meaning of life. It is sadly true that man has not always
assented gracefully to the right answers to his questions —
even when they have been forthcoming. Desperate minds,
nonetheless, have searched after God in the hope that they
might find him (Acts 17). No man has found true peace of
mind or heart until he has been able to answer the questions,
How can I know God? How am I to understand myself?
What is my proper relationship to God? These are the very
questions which revelation seeks to answer. No small wonder
is it then that modern man cannot ignore this crucial topic.[2]

The current debate over revelation reflects also the theological bankruptcy of the mid-twentieth century. Orthodoxy
has lost its grip upon the minds of men. Modernism has
finally spent its strength; and at least in the form in which
it has previously exhibited itself, it is no longer a live option.
To the present moment no alternative has proved capable
of capturing and holding the allegiance of modern man.
Hearts and minds therefore are empty, and men are without
direction or meaning for life. As C. J. Jung puts it, "Side by
side with the decline of religious life, the neuroses grow
noticeably more frequent. Everywhere the mental state of
European men shows an alarming lack of balance. We are
living undoubtedly in a period of the greatest restlessness,
nervous tension, confusion and disorientation of outlook.
. . . Everyone of them has the feeling that our modern
religious truths have somehow or other grown empty." [3]

The American theologian Nels Ferré documents this
personal crisis in the religious life of one of his own students:
"One of the ablest and most thoughtful students in my
seminar recently expressed his problem thus: 'If I simply
accept faith and then reason out what follows from there,

I cannot feel sure of myself. How do I know that I am not just rationalizing? If, however, I insist on justifying my faith by reason, it seems to me that I have no faith. In one case I am arbitrary and have nothing to say to all the people who start from another faith and refuse to examine it. In the other case I have no hope and driving power for a world like this!' " [4]

The predicament of the student is that of many thinking people throughout the world. Anyone who has lost his faith in the authority of the Bible must inevitably ask, What is truth? What shall I believe? How can I know whether this doctrine or the opposite doctrine is true? A deep pall of skepticism hangs threateningly over the heads of all who do not possess the authority of divine revelation. [5]

The surging tide of debate about revelation, therefore, proves not only that the topic of revelation is of perennial and crucial significance to mankind; it also proves that modern man, in particular, having strayed from the revelation that was his in the past, is today lost, without God and without hope in the world.

This double significance of the contemporary debate over revelation calls imperatively for evangelical Christians to speak forth boldly and earnestly upon the issues of today. Men are confused and willing to listen. They are restless and searching for answers to their desperate questions. They are determined to find an answer — some answer — any answer.

Seeking to resolve these uncertainties, Christians down through the centuries have pointed to the Bible. The Bible alone, they testify, points unerringly to Jesus Christ as Saviour. The Bible alone is the infallible rule of faith and practice. It alone can speak with the authority of the omniscient God Himself. It alone can tell man what he ought to believe, and what he ought to do. And in it alone can man find full assurance for his faith so that he dares affirm, "I know what I believe."

Long ago St. Augustine (c. A.D. 400), searching desperately for truth to lighten the gloom of ancient skepticism, turned to the Scriptures and found in them peace of mind and heart. Of this book he exclaimed, "As to all other writings . . . I do not accept their teaching as true on the mere ground of the opinion being held by them; but . . . these canonical writings . . . are free from error." [6]

The testimony of Augustine is the testimony of the united voice of the ancient church. From Irenaeus to Billy Graham the orthodox Christian faith has stood unequivocally for the divine inspiration and inerrant authority of Scripture. The forthright claim of Gaussen, made over a hundred years ago, has never been successfully challenged: "With the single exception of Theodore of Mopsuestia (c. A.D. 400), that philosophical divine whose numerous writings were condemned for their Nestorianism in the fifth ecumenical council . . . it has been found impossible to produce in the long course of the first eight centuries of Christianity a single doctor who had disowned the plenary inspiration of the Scriptures, unless it be in the bosom of the most violent heresies." [7]

Luther took his place in the main stream of historic Christianity when he declared, "Holy Scriptures cannot err." [8] Calvin was no less explicit in his reference to the Bible as the "pure word of God," and as the "infallible rule of His holy truth." [9] This same conviction as to the authority of the Bible found its expression in all the great creeds of classical Protestantism.[10]

It has been echoed and re-echoed in the time-honored question of the ordination ceremony: "Do you believe the

Scriptures of the Old and New Testaments to be the Word of God, the only infallible rule of faith and practice?"

Beginning in the eighteenth century, however, this doctrine has come under increasing attack. Although few cared to put the matter so bluntly, most modern theologians agreed in essence with Hendrick Van Loon when he wrote, "The Old Testament was a national Jewish scrapbook. It contained stories and legends and genealogies and love poems and songs, classified and arranged and re-classified and re-arranged without any regard for chronological order or literary perfection." [11]

Such a view of the origin of the Bible is, of course, utterly incompatible with the traditional doctrine of its divine inspiration and authority. In his *Outline of Biblical Theology*, Millar Burrows accurately summarizes the typical modern viewpoint: "The Bible is full of things which to an intelligent educated person of today are either quite incredible, or at best highly questionable. From the account of creation in the first chapter of Genesis to the description of the heavenly city in the closing chapters of Revelation, statements abound that even the most tortuous interpretations cannot reconcile with the modern scientific conception of the universe . . . The protracted struggle of theology to defend the inerrancy of the Bible against the findings of astronomy, geology and biology has been a series of retreats ending in a defeat which has led all wise theologians to move to a better position." [12]

On the positive side, modern thinkers tended to regard the Bible as a more or less historical account (rather less than more) of the development of religious life in a particular nation with a genius for God. For them the Bible was the story of men who attained a successful religious experience and in their writings passed on their best insights to posterity. The apex of this development was to be found in Jesus Christ, the greatest genius of them all. To Him they would accord even the honorific titles: "Saviour" (because He has helped us the most) and "Lord" (because He is the best authority). During the nineteenth century such views of the inspiration and authority of the Bible gradually spread throughout the nominal Christian church both in Europe and in America. By the first third of the twentieth century these views had become almost universally accepted in the leading theological schools on both continents.

Suddenly, however, at the zenith of its influence the whole structure of modern theology fell apart. Although its leaders sincerely attempted to remain within the structure of Christian tradition, it became increasingly obvious as time went by that Modernism had made a radical break with all that was essential to earlier Protestant faith. Emil Brunner only echoed the substance of fundamentalist apologetic when he declared, "[Anyone] possessed of a reasonably correct knowledge of Christianity, will have little difficulty in proving that the modernist teaches, under the label of Christianity, a religion that has nothing in common with Christianity except a few words, and that those words cover concepts which are irreconcilable with the content of Christian faith." [13]

The most obvious predicament of Modernism was its lack of authority. In the time-honored custom of preaching, a Bible which had become a mere scrapbook of Jewish devotional material could do well enough in a pinch as a source book for sermon texts, but such a Bible was totally unfitted for proclamation in ancient prophetic style, "Thus saith the Lord."

Karl Barth relates how in the early days of his ministry he gradually became disillusioned with the milk-toast "good advice," which was all he had to offer his parishioners. Faced with the realities of war, he discovered to his consternation that he possessed only a frothy palaver of superficial guesses. As he mounted the pulpit Sunday mornings to deliver his sermons, the table of the law slipped between his fingers. He stood before his people a mere man pleading a man's wisdom which even he only half believed.[14]

As the religious bankruptcy of Modernism became more and more obvious, disillusioned leaders began to look back with nostalgia upon historic Protestantism with its strong note of authority and its comforting gospel for sinners. "Our grandfathers, after all, were right," Barth declares, "when they struggled so desperately for the truth that there is revelation in the Bible and our fathers were right when they guarded warily against being drawn out upon the shaky scaffolding of religious self-expression. We live in a sick old world which cries out from its soul out of deep need, 'Heal me, O Lord, and I will be healed.' And for all men whoever and whatever and wherever they may be, there is a longing for exactly this which is within the Bible." [15]

In the last few decades a new theological movement has appeared upon the horizon and indeed has conquered the field. The "strange new world within the Bible" first discovered by Karl Barth back in 1916 is now no longer either new or strange, but has made for itself a large place in the sun. Neo-orthodoxy has superseded Modernism as the dominant theology in mid-twentieth century and with it has come an entirely new view of the Bible — yet not new, so its enthusiasts assert, but the old view rediscovered — the view of the Bible set forth in the classical Protestantism of the reformers.

This return to the authority of the Bible is by no means to be misconstrued as a return to the fundamentalist view. The Neo-orthodox revolt against the liberal reduction of the

Bible to a mere human word of religious advice is at the
same time accompanied by severe criticism of traditional
orthodoxy.

Brunner asserts bluntly, "The orthodox doctrine of verbal
inspiration has been finally destroyed. It is clear that there
is no connection between it and scientific research and
honesty. We are forced to make a decision for or against
this view." [16] He further explains his own departure from
Fundamentalism by adding, "I myself am an adherent of a
rather radical school of Biblical criticism which for example,
does not accept the Gospel of John as an historical source
and finds much to be objected to in many parts of the
synoptic gospels . . . the theology of the apostles is not an
absolute entity but is presented in a series of different types
of doctrines which differ considerably from one another." [17]

Karl Barth, usually less belligerent against Fundamentalism
than Brunner, makes the same point clear. "Where the
Bible is held up as a collection of authoritative documents
and witnesses, its human element must be denied or over-
looked. The human features of the Bible must then become
a shame, and man is called upon for a sacrifice of the
intellect." [18] The orthodox view is not only ruled out on
grounds of our modern scientific knowledge, but it is not
even the view which the Bible presents of itself. "It is,"
declares Barth, "a noteworthy contradiction that those who
wish to raise the Bible to this height are in fact not true to
the Bible. The Bible itself claims something quite different
for itself." Therefore the orthodox who seem to hold such
a high view of the complete truth and inspiration of the
Bible, are in reality setting themselves against the teaching of
the Bible. Any truly Biblical theologian, Barth therefore insists, must repudiate the orthodox position just because he *is*
Biblical.[18]

The fundamental objection of the Neo-orthodox against traditional orthodoxy is their conviction that Christ, not the Bible, is the proper object of religious faith. Fundamentalists, they say, reverse this order, thereby erecting the Bible into an idol. For them belief in the Bible comes first; and because they believe the Bible, they also profess to believe in Christ. On the contrary, the right basis for belief, so the Neo-orthodox affirm, is Christ first. And then to the degree that the Bible witnesses to the living Christ, they accept the Bible. In his *Christian Doctrine of God* Brunner seeks to put the Biblical writings in their proper place. "That means," he explains, "that their witness can never be the basis and object of faith, but only a means of faith. We do not believe in Jesus Christ because we first of all believe in the story and teaching of the apostles, but by means of the testimony of their narrative we believe as they do and in a similar state of freedom. Faith in Jesus Christ is not based upon a previous faith in the Bible, but it is based solely upon the witness of the Holy Spirit." Protestant orthodoxy, therefore, which professes so glibly to be the guardian of the true faith, has in reality turned aside to an idolatrous form of Christianity.[19]

In their view of the authority of Holy Scripture, the Neo-orthodox are united in their opposition to Modernism and Fundamentalism, but the same cannot be said of their positive attempts to construct a new view of the Bible. They are, nonetheless, in remarkable agreement upon the main outlines of their understanding of the inspiration of the Bible and of the nature of its authority. One of the basic and most tenaciously held convictions of the Neo-orthodox theologians is that revelation can never be a body of truth or set of propositions. It is always an act or event in which God discloses His person. In an authoritative article in Kittel's *Theologisches Wörterbuch*, the German scholar

Albrecht Oepke writes, "Revelation is not the communication of rational knowledge and not the stimulation of numinous [a sense of God] . . . feelings. In itself, however, revelation is neither of these things, but is quite essentially a transaction of Yahweh — an unveiling of his essential hiddenness — His offering of Himself in mutual fellowship." [20]

Emil Brunner defends the same viewpoint: "In the time of the apostles as in that of the Old Testament prophets, divine revelation always meant the whole of the divine activity for the salvation of the world. Divine revelation is not a book or a doctrine. Revelation is God Himself in His self-manifestation within history. Revelation is something that happens." [21]

In accordance with this deep-seated conviction that revelation is the personal activity of God and never an interpretation of truth, the Neo-orthodox rule out the Bible as a revelation from God. The Bible, rather, is a record of revelation. It tells the story of what God has done in history to reveal Himself. It relates the testimonies of men to whom God has revealed Himself in the past. The Bible represents a human attempt to understand and to bear witness to the revelatory works of God.

As a human record of revelation, the Bible can by no means be infallible. Barth declares, "The prophets and apostles even as such, even in their office, even in their function as witnesses, even in the action of writing down their testimonies were really historically, and therefore in their deeds, sinful, and in their spoken and written word capable of error and actually erring men like us all." [22]

The Bible, however, is not *merely* a book which contains the Word of God. It also in God's sovereignty becomes the instrument through which men experience a contemporary revelation of God in their own souls. Just as He spoke to the

Biblical witnesses long ago, so today God's Spirit works upon the hearts and minds of men to speak to them from the pages of Scripture. By this act of divine inspiration the Bible here and now becomes the contemporary, living Word of God, calling men into fellowship with Himself.

The Neo-orthodox view of Scripture is thus best understood by an analogy with a sermon. A sermon is obviously a human production, which may contain errors. The pastor may miss the date in his literary reference to Caesar's crossing of the Rubicon. He may, in fact, display deplorable mistakes in exegesis. He may fall into grievous doctrinal errors. In spite of blunders, even a pulpit tyro may deliver a useful sermon, which may lead man to Jesus Christ and the revelation of God.

Indirectly, the sermon may even be called the Word of God. We do not mean that every word of the sermon is composed of words given by God, but notwithstanding literary flaws and doctrinal errors here and there, the sermon sets forth the gospel of Jesus Christ clearly enough so that men may hear it, understand it, receive it, and be saved. So Barth recognizes the Bible to be the Word of God. "That sinful and erring men as such spoke the Word of God, that is the miracle of which we speak when we say the Bible is God's word." [23]

The analogy between a sermon and the Bible as conceived by the Neo-orthodox can be carried one step farther. A man frequently hears a sermon only with his ears, but does nothing about it; for to him it does not actually unveil Jesus Christ as a Saviour. Then suddenly the message of the sermon strikes home. Jesus Christ is unveiled to him. The impotent human word spoken by the preacher is no longer impotent, but becomes in truth God's word to him. So the Bible becomes God's word when God actually speaks to man in and through the words of the Bible. And as He speaks it, this Bible is God's word.[24]

For the Neo-orthodox, finally, this erring human Bible, which may become God's word, is also the ultimate authority for man's religious life. The extent of Biblical authority is conceived in radically different ways by various Neo-orthodox thinkers. Some find the authority of the Bible only in its inmost message and then disagree as to what that message really is. For Rudolph Bultmann and Reinhold Niebuhr it is the message of the absolute self-giving love of God for man, the sinner. This absolute love is set forth in the Biblical "myth" of Christ's atoning death. Here, mythologically speaking, God takes to Himself the sin of man and so forgives man freely.[25]

For Emil Brunner, on the other hand, the authority of the Bible centers about what it tells of the Christ, the God-man. Unfortunately Brunner never defines precisely what he thinks are the limits of Biblical authority; and, accordingly, his dependence upon it varies greatly from one passage of his writings to another.[26]

For Karl Barth, the most conservative Neo-orthodox thinker, the Bible is the standard of all right teaching and all right thinking about God. The Bible, no doubt, contains errors; but those errors do not negate Biblical authority. If God condescends to speak to men in and through fallible words, Barth queries, why should any man be so proud that he is unwilling to hear what God has to say? Is man more fastidious than God? "In spite of apparent human defects," Barth declares forcibly, "God now speaks what this text speaks." And he adds, "Everything which is here to be said can be put together in the sentence: 'The faith in the inspiration of the Bible stands or falls with this, that the concrete life of the church and members of the church is a life ruled by the exegesis of the Bible.' " [27] The Bible taken as a whole, therefore, is the authority for the church, the final court of appeal in faith and practice.

As a result of this new trend in contemporary theology, an atmosphere of uncertainty and indecision has been created within the ranks of evangelical Christianity. Battle lines have become exceedingly confused. Not precise definitions, but rather foggy and misleading generalizations are the fashion of our day. Theological discussions are often carried on under conditions of exceedingly low intellectual and spiritual visibility. In the confusion and heat of the battle, some evangelicals have fearfully suggested that we must reconstruct the whole of the evangelical position with respect to the Bible and its inspiration and authority. Others, equally fearful, have sought to harden the clichés of a past generation in its battle against Modernism and they refuse to examine their inherited convictions in the light of contemporary thinking. Sad to say, these men sometimes think that it is more important to be against Barth than for Biblical truth.

A true and living orthodoxy must never become static. If we are to remain faithful to the orthodox faith of our fathers, we dare not merely repeat our fathers' answers to opponents of a generation ago. A living orthodoxy, rather, must rethink for its own generation the doctrines of revelation and inspiration. It must be prepared to fight on the battle lines as they are drawn today, and must appropriate the truth of God as it has been given. Certainly no Christian need ever fear the honest search for truth in humble dependence upon the illumination of the Holy Spirit.

In his re-examination of Biblical authority in the light of contemporary debate, however, the evangelical Christian is not like a rudderless ship floating aimlessly upon a boundless

sea, driven and tossed by every passing wind. He is bound
by the same hard core of revelational facts which have
determined orthodox thinking in the past. By no means does
he consider these facts to be an infringement upon his
freedom to think realistically, constructively, and honestly.
A tough-minded, even literal, adherence to every least fact
provided by the data of revelation is the only possible foundation for clear and effective thinking about God and man's
relationship to God. To rethink, therefore, is not necessarily
to throw overboard the orthodox view of Biblical authority;
rather, it is to constitute it a true and living *orthodoxy*
(straight thinking and teaching).

In the light of the contemporary debate about revelation
and authority the Biblical position may be outlined in the
following points:

1. *The ultimate object of all Biblical revelation is God as
a person.*

All revelation has God for its object. The Bible does not
present man with a set of universal truths like the propositions of Euclid in geometry. It does not set forth in formal
fashion the arguments and counter-arguments of a theological
textbook. No creedal formulations — certainly not the fundamental doctrines of the older liberal theology, such as the
universal fatherhood of God, the universal brotherhood of
man, and the supremacy of love — are the focus of Biblical
revelation.

The ultimate goal of revelation is not so much to make
man wise as it is to bring him into a direct encounter with
God as a person, and to evoke from him a response of love
and obedience to God. The Apostle Paul sets forth the
goal of all revelation: "That I may be personally acquainted
with him" (Phil. 3:10).[28]

2. *Biblical revelation is by divine acts.*

Biblical revelation is the unfolding of the gracious acts of God in behalf of sinful man. From the skin of a slain animal with which God sought to cover the shame of our first parents, to the vision of the heavenly city in Revelation 22, the long course of Biblical history is the story of what God has done for His people — the righteous acts of Jehovah (Micah 6:5 ARV).

3. *Biblical revelation culminates in Jesus Christ.*

In the "fulness of time" came Jesus Christ (Gal. 4:4). "God . . . hath . . . spoken unto us by His Son" (Heb. 1:1). The supreme act by which God reveals Himself is by His incarnation. God became man, lived as man, died for man, and rose again from the dead. Indeed, the story of these events is good *news* — news about something which happened in the land of Palestine during the reigns of Augustus and Tiberius Caesar. It is news of what Christ did on Calvary (I Cor. 15:1–4). There God performed His mightiest act by giving Himself for the redemption of lost humanity (Luke 20:9ff.).

The Bible preserves an important distinction between Christ as redeemer and Christ as revealer. In both of these roles Jesus Christ is supreme. As redeemer, however, Christ is not merely supreme over all other modes of redemption. His uniqueness is absolute. Like Christ, the prophets also spoke; but the prophets did not redeem. As revealer, Christ's uniqueness lies in the completeness and finality of His revelation. Others beside Him spoke the Word of God; but He was, in truth, *God speaking.*[29]

4. *Biblical revelation is also divine interpretation of meaning.*

That God reveals Himself as a person and that He does so by His acts does not preclude the fact that God also reveals truth about Himself. According to the Scriptures, man is responsible for knowing who God is (Deut. 6:4; Matt. 16:13), and what is His will (Lev. 20:7), and what are His plans and goals (Mark 16:15). These truths man must know in order rightly and effectively to know the person of God and to enter into obedient fellowship with Him. Our Lord spoke with luminous insight into the needs of the human heart when he declared, "the truth shall make you free" (John 8:32).

To those outside the framework of strict orthodoxy, few see this more clearly than does Edwin Lewis. "Revelation," Lewis argues, "means that God is categorically affirmed and that He bears a certain character and that He is working for certain ends; and what these ends are, likewise, is included in the revelation. God utters His Word, but the meaning of what is uttered is still to be conveyed and this is the work of the Holy Spirit. Revelation brings a disclosure of truth which would otherwise have remained at best only a speculation." [30]

According to the teaching of Scripture, therefore, God reveals to man truths or propositions about Himself and His will, about ourselves and our needs, and about His provision and care and promise of grace. Thus in First Corinthians 2:9–12 and 16 we read:

Eye hath not seen, nor ear heard, neither have entered into the heart of man the things which God hath prepared for them that love him. (10) But God hath revealed them unto us by his spirit: for the spirit searcheth all things, yea the deep things of God. (11) For what man knoweth the things of a man save the spirit of man which is in him? Even so the things of God knoweth no man, but the Spirit of God. (12) Now we have received, not the spirit of the world, but the spirit which is of God; that we might know the things that are freely given to us of God. (16) For who hath known the mind of the Lord, that he might instruct Him? But we have the mind of Christ.

The flow of Paul's thought is inescapable. God has certain plans for those who love Him. These plans are, of course, quite unknown and undiscoverable by man. Just as man can know what is in his own mind, however, so the Spirit of God knows fully the truth lying within the divine mind, and out of love and grace chooses to convey this otherwise inaccessible truth to the minds of men. The process whereby this communication of divine truth takes place is specifically labeled as revelation.

Other New Testament passages bear out the same idea. Matthew 11:22 gives us revealed truth regarding God's future judgment. Unto the Jews, declares the Apostle Paul, "were committed the oracles of God" (Rom. 3:2). In the third chapter of Ephesians the same apostle refers to the revealed truth that Jews and Gentiles are to be one body. In Matthew 16:17 the revealed truth is that Jesus Christ is the Son of God, and in Luke 2:26 the revelation (*chrematidzo*) brings to Simeon truth as to his own destiny.[31]

In the Old Testament we find a similar pattern of thought. In the third chapter of First Samuel the writer ascribes to God a revelation of the truth about Samuel's call. The Old Testament prophets often claimed that God had revealed to them secrets (Amos 3:7 and Dan. 2). Special propositional communications from God are frequently labeled as revealed truths (Isa. 22:14, Dan. 2:29, 30, II Sam. 7:27).

The hesitation of Neo-orthodox thinkers to accept the unequivocal claims of Scripture in support of revelation in and through a divinely given interpretation of meaning is indeed strange, coming from those who pride themselves upon their "Biblical theology." The God of most contemporary theologians can act but does not speak. Prophetic testimony becomes no longer "the more sure word of prophecy" given forth with divine authority (II Pet. 1:19–21). It is reduced to mere private interpretation stemming from the will of man. Human insight thus replaces divine truth.

The God of the Bible is very different from this concept. He is the God who acts! He is also the God who speaks to His servants. "The Biblical writers," so C. H. Dodd reminds us, "were not philosophers constructing a speculative theory from their observation of events. What they said was 'Thus saith the Lord'; and they firmly believed that God spoke to men. The interpretation of history which they offered was not invented by process of thought; it was the meaning which they experienced in the events when their minds were open to God as well as open to the impact of outward facts. Thus the prophetic interpretation of history and the impetus and direction which that gave to subsequent history were alike the Word of God to men." [32]

An inductive study of the Scriptures, therefore, leads inevitably to the conclusion that Biblical revelation includes divine revelation of truth. The all but unanimous view of contemporary theologians that Biblical revelation is personal and through acts, but never propositional, simply will not bear the test of exegesis. It is true that God reveals Himself as a person; and it is true that He does so through acts. But it is also true that God gives specific revelation of truth to His prophets and apostles. He is a living, acting, speaking person who enters into social intercourse and fellowship with man and who gives to men a revelation, His own divine interpretation of the meaning of things.

5. *This revelation is brought to men by the Bible.*

The redemptive acts of God together with the divine interpretation of these mighty acts were recorded in the writings of the apostles and prophets. The Bible thus becomes the means through which revelations given directly to prophets in Old Testament history and to apostles in New Testament history are made available for the needy sinner of every succeeding generation. In this sense is to be found the element of truth contained in the oft-repeated phrase, "The Bible contains the Word of God."

The central message of both Testaments is, of course, Jesus Christ. In the Old Testament is to be found the preparatory revelation. Our Lord Himself declared that the Scriptures testify of Him (John 5:39). He rebuked those who did not find Him in the Old Testament for their failure to understand the sacred text (Luke 24:25).

In perfect harmony with the claims of Christ as to the central message of the Old Testament, the apostle John revealed the purpose of his gospel. "These are written that ye might believe that Jesus is the Christ, the Son of God, and that believing ye might have life through his name" (John 20:31).

The primary purpose of the whole Bible, therefore, is that man may come to know Jesus Christ, the living Word of God. It is a book which tells about Him and which brings to men of every age the revelation which God has given as to the meaning of Jesus Christ for lost sinners.

6. *Revelation must be subjectively appropriated.*

The objective side of the divine work of revelation needs to be supplemented by an internal subjective work of the Spirit of God. In the past the orthodox have usually referred to this subjective work by the term *illumination*. The Bible, of course, does not speak in the language of the classroom, and therefore does not preserve this nice distinction between revelation (Old Testament, *galah*; New Testament, *apoka-lupto*) and illumination.

In I Samuel 3:7, for example, we read: "Now Samuel did not yet know the Lord. Neither was the Word of the Lord yet revealed unto him." From the context we learn that God had already spoken, but Samuel had not yet perceived that Word as from God. In one sense the word was uncovered objectively but in another sense it was not yet subjectively uncovered for Samuel himself.

Both of these concepts, subjective revelation and objective revelation or illumination, are introduced without being named specifically in the classic passage, I Corinthians 2. God gave a revelation to His chosen apostle. In this case the revelation is not merely a divine act, but an act to convey truth from the mind of God to the apostle. With divine sanction and authority this revealed truth is in turn conveyed by the apostle to others. The natural man, however, whose mind is darkened by sin, cannot receive as true the message which God revealed. He needs the illumination of the Holy Spirit so that he can really see what is there available for him. In short, from the Biblical point of view, man needs subjective illumination so that what has been objectively revealed in the past and brought to him objectively through the inspiration of the prophets may become subjectively revealed to him personally.

The cliché, "The Bible *becomes* the Word of God," thus has a significant element of truth in it. The Biblical message came from God whether men receive it as such or whether they do not, but now and again the Spirit of God takes the words of the Bible and makes them subjectively the Word

of God to individual men. Instead of the dead letter of the
law, the Bible thereby becomes the living voice of the Spirit
in the heart of men. It becomes God's contemporary message, spanning in an instant the millennia between the prophet
of old and the man of today.[33]

7. *The authority of the Bible is known by revelation.*

Once it is granted that the Bible *contains* the Word of God,
it immediately becomes important to ascertain what this
divine word found in the Bible has to say about the place
of the Bible in the life of the believer. If, for example, the
Bible provides for us a reliable record of the revelation of
Jesus Christ as God incarnate, then it is obvious that we
cannot stop at this point. Once we are committed to the
Lordship of Jesus Christ, we must immediately accept also
the authority of the Bible; for we discover that our Lord
Himself accepted its authority and taught His followers to
do likewise. To admit that Jesus is Lord, but to reject His
instruction as to the authority of the Bible is, to put the
matter bluntly, little more than pious self-deception.

In similar fashion, if we accept the claims of the apostles
and prophets for the divine origin and authority of their
message, we must accordingly receive their conclusions with
respect to the authority of the Bible when that constitutes
part of their message. To acknowledge the claims of the
Biblical writers that they are transmitting to us not their
own word but the Word of God, and then to ignore what
that Word has to say about the authority of their own writings, is illogical.

Modern thinkers have resorted to all sorts of desperate
expedients in order to circumvent this simple conclusion. It
is, so some suggest, an argument in a circle: Major premise:
Whatever the Bible teaches is true; Minor premise: The

Bible teaches that it is true; Conclusion: Therefore, the Bible must be true.[34] If the basis for belief in the deity of Christ and for belief in the doctrinal authority of the prophets and apostles depended first upon our prior belief in the verbal inspiration of the Bible or in its inerrant authority, then the charge of a circular argument could stand. Such, however, is not the case.

Belief in the deity of Christ rests in part upon the whole sum of historical, logical, and experiential evidences that validate to men the truth of Christian faith. These evidences, moreover, are brought home to the human heart and mind as God creates in His elect a certainty of the truth of Christ through the witness of His Holy Spirit working immediately and directly upon the human mind.

Likewise the authority of the apostles and prophets rests upon their relationship to Jesus Christ and upon the trustworthiness of their testimony concerning the divine origin of their message. Since, therefore, our confidence in Christ and in the validity of the revelation contained in the Scriptures rests not upon our belief in the divine inspiration of these writings but upon objective evidences and, especially, upon the internal testimony of the Holy Spirit, the charge of arguing in a circle cannot stand.

Other opponents of Biblical authority, with more show of logic, argue that the Scriptures may contain revelation but also contain what is merely human speculation. The teachings of the Bible about its own authority fall into the latter category of the human element rather than that derived from divine revelation. Such an argument, however, does not apply to the testimony of Christ. If Jesus Christ is the divine Lord, then insofar as the gospel writers accurately record His words, we are bound to receive all that

He taught and commanded us to receive. Anything less than this is to do despite to Him as Lord of our lives.

The Bible is so full and deep in its teaching on the authority of Scripture that all who argue this way are placed in an impossible dilemma. Either the Biblical writers are utterly untrustworthy in their claims that they have received authority to teach from God; or, if their claims are valid at all, they are certainly true at this point. There is no other question on which the apostolic writers are in such clear agreement or on which they speak with more freedom or assurance than upon the doctrine of the authority of the Scriptures.[35]

The Biblical teaching as to the completeness of its authority is so obvious that to discuss it here may seem superfluous. In His sermon on the mount (Matt. 5:17–19) our Lord declared, "One jot or one tittle shall in no wise pass from the law." He rebuked His disciples for not believing "all that the prophets had spoken" (Luke 24:25). In controversy with the Jews (John 10:35) He argued, "Scripture cannot be broken [dissolved or discarded]." On one occasion He introduced an isolated passage of the Old Testament with the formula "God says" (Matt. 19:5). In the thought and teaching of our Lord the law of Moses is explicitly labeled the "Word of God" (Mark 7:6ff).

Just at this point is to be found the Achilles' heel of the Neo-orthodox. By appealing from the written Scripture to a voice of the Spirit they are in effect setting themselves above the Bible. They put the Bible into a sieve and receive from it only what sifts through. The sieves used may vary greatly. One who uses a sieve with large holes receives much of the Bible. Another uses such a fine sieve that practically nothing of Scripture filters through to him.

Karl Barth thus seems inconsistent when he decries the rejection of Biblical authority evidenced by American left-wing Neo-orthodox theologians. They "theologize on their own account," charges Barth, "that is to say, without asking on what Biblical grounds one puts forward this or that professedly Christian view. They would quote the Bible according to choice, according as it appeared to them to strengthen their own view and without feeling any need to ask whether the words quoted really have in their context the meaning attributed to them." The Bible, in short, is for them no true authority; and Barth adds that "to this irresponsible attitude toward the Bible" he is "irrevocably opposed." [37] To this testimony of Barth we can only reply, "*Et tu, Brute!*"

In similar fashion a liberal critic of Reinhold Niebuhr declares, "Niebuhr claims to base his faith on the Bible and calls it Biblical faith, but a careful examination shows that he corrects the Bible according to his own convictions. According to Niebuhr many of the truths of the Bible are presented in the form of myths, but myths are defective, he admits, and even Jesus and Paul were deceived by them. When Niebuhr corrects the errors of the Biblical authorities, I think Niebuhr points out that Niebuhr's faith is determined by himself and not by the Bible. Niebuhr may be right and the Bible wrong, but I should like to hear what Jesus and Paul had to say in their own defense before pronouncing Niebuhr right and Jesus and Paul mistaken about the Christian faith." [38]

When, on the contrary, Billy Graham stands up to preach, he declares: "The Bible says . . ." By this twentieth-century equivalent of the apostolic, "It is written," he clearly intends that what the Bible says is not merely his opinion, or that of a first-century sage, but it is the truth of God coming with the authority of God Himself. This unshakable conviction that in the Bible God has spoken and, therefore, that the Bible message possesses divine authority, transforms the Christian evangelist from a purveyor of good advice into a divinely commissioned ambassador of Jesus Christ.

8. *The authority of the Bible is derived from its divine inspiration.*

Referring to the Old Testament, the Apostle Paul declares, "All Scripture [is] given by inspiration," literally "breathed out" or given forth by God. In this divine giving of the Scripture Paul finds the explanation for the fact that it is "profitable for doctrine, for reproof, for correction, for instruction in righteousness: that the man of God may be throughly furnished" (II Tim. 3:16, 17).

The Apostle Peter likewise explains why Scripture is a "more sure word of prophecy" by basing its authority on its origin. The prophets of old did not give their personal interpretation of the events which they describe, but rather they were moved by the Holy Ghost so that what they said derived ultimately from God (II Peter 1:19–21). The Apostle does not teach that the Bible was dictated by God but rather that it was produced by the prophets through a divine energizing and enabling, the precise nature of which is not described, but the effect of which was to constitute the prophetic writings God's divinely authoritative message to men.

Karl Barth strongly objects to this understanding of the nature of Biblical inspiration. He refers to it as a "denial of the humanity" of Scripture demanding of us a "sacrifice of the intellect." [39] Our Lord and His apostles, however, did not envisage any such drastic antinomy between a human authorship and a divine control and production of Scripture.

The human qualities in Scripture are properly recognized, but in and through the human authors of Scripture God's guiding hand produced the writings He wished in order to convey His thoughts to men. It is this "divine plus" of which the apostles speak when they refer to the inspiration of the Bible by God and seek in this inspiration to explain the true authority of Scripture.

This view of the inspiration and authority of the Bible is quite obviously what is traditionally known as verbal inspiration. Unfortunately the term has been misunderstood. It means the work of the Holy Spirit by which, without setting aside the personality and literary talents of its human authors, He guided the writers of Scripture so that the words of the Bible in its entirety unfold His divinely written Word to men and therefore teach the truth without error.[40]

The method by which this inspiration was accomplished is, of course, scarcely referred to in Scripture and is certainly not discussed at length. The *fact* of the inspiration of Scripture by God and *its consequent authority* are of vital importance to the Scriptural writers. The mechanics of inspiration are left unexplained. To argue that a divine inspiration must necessarily negate the freedom and humanity of the Biblical writers is scarcely possible for one who pretends to be a Christian. Whatever may be said for or against a rational solution of this problem, it ought to be abundantly clear that no theist who believes in God's providential control of the universe can possibly use this objection against the inspiration of the Bible. The God of Romans 8:28, who works all things together for good, including the sinful acts of wicked men, could certainly have worked through the will and personality of His prophets to secure the divine Word which He wished to convey through them.

9. *The Bible must be rightly interpreted.*

A Biblical view of inspiration does not rule out either historical or textual criticism. Rather it demands legitimate application of these studies to a proper understanding of the Bible. In the science of higher criticism, for example, the Christian scholar investigates the origin, authorship, genuineness, date, and authenticity of the various books of the Bible. It is an obvious fact that one who concludes that the book of Deuteronomy was a sixth-century fraud foisted upon a superstitious king by pious forgers can scarcely hold to the inspiration and divine authority of that book. The Biblical view does not rule out higher criticism, but it does rule out certain conclusions to which many higher critics have come; namely, all those conclusions contradicting anything taught in the original words of Scripture or assuming that only a human author, not God, is responsible for the words of Scripture.

By the scientific use of the correct principles of lower criticism, likewise, the reverent scholar is able in most instances to ascertain the original text of Scripture. In the introduction to their Greek New Testament, Westcott and Hort declare that except for differences in spelling and trivial variations having no effect on the teaching of the passage, the words of our present text about which there can be any reasonable doubt form hardly more than a thousandth part of the whole.[41]

The correct text thus secured serves as a reliable basis for exegetical study, and its faithful interpretation provides man with the very Word of God. Only by holding a completely authoritative original can one have confidence that he has the truth of God which comes to him with divine authority.

Were it not for the doctrine of the infallible authority of the original manuscripts, one could never be sure, even after he had finished the task of textual criticism, that he had anything more than a mere man's opinion as to what is the truth.

Unfortunately the Bible frequently suffers much from misinterpretation. To hold to the complete authority of the Bible does not by any means commit one to say that God approved of all unethical practices mentioned in the Bible; nor does it mean that every statement quoted in Scripture is true, for in Psalm 14 we find the words, "There is no God." The author of Scripture obviously does not endorse this blasphemy, but correctly ascribes it to the fool. Inspiration does not guarantee that Scripture gives us specific technical data in current scientific vocabulary. Scripture speaks, rather, in the language of the common man of two or more millennia ago, but what it speaks it speaks truthfully, whether it deals with ethics or with the natural world of science.

The question at issue is always: What is really the teaching of Scripture? No doubt some very foolish things have been said at this point. The King James Bible has been made to substantiate all sorts of strange scientific theories. No doubt those who point back to an infallible original have sometimes placed an almost magical interpretation upon the Scripture so as to transform it from a book of faith and practice into a scientific textbook suitable for a course in biology. This is to misinterpret the message of the Bible, and to make it say what it does not intend to say at all.

Adequate Biblical interpretation, moreover, does not preclude the use of figurative, allegorical, and symbolical language. It does not guarantee that two Biblical writers describing the same event may not avail themselves of very different, and to a superficial reader, discrepant words. It does mean that the words of Scripture are studied faithfully in their total context in order to discover the thought which God seeks to communicate to the minds of men. He who would learn of God is not to seek to go behind the Scripture in his interpretation of it. He is not to seek some message of God suggested to him upon the basis of the Scripture. He is to go to the Scripture, place himself under its lordship, and seek to discover exactly what it teaches. When he has discovered what Scripture teaches, precisely this is the message of God for him, which comes to him with all the authority of God Himself and calls forth from man an existential response of obedience or of disobedience to the Word of God.

10. *The fact of Biblical authority is the foundation for a valid theology.*

Once more the question comes back to the basic issue: What think ye of Christ? And to this question we must add also: What shall we do about the prophetic and apostolic claim to authority?

This decision of history flows from an inner logic deep within the structure of Christian faith. Some short-sighted individuals may inquire, "Why not accept the inner essence of Christianity, its gospel of Christ, but reject the troublesome doctrine of the complete authority of Scripture?" How can this be done? The truth of Christianity and the authority of the Bible stand or fall together. Recent scholarship, radical as well as conservative, has tended more and more to agree that Jesus, the man of history, believed unequivocally in the ordinary view of the inspiration and authority of the Scripture held by the Jewish people of His day. Even more unanimous is the conclusion that the apostolic writers were in essential agreement with their Jewish opponents in accepting the complete authority of the Old Testament.[42]

To accept Christ as Lord and to submit to His teaching regarding the complete authority of Scripture is consistent. Again, to acknowledge the validity of apostolic claims to authority and to receive their teaching as to the complete authority of Scripture is also consistent. To accept Christ's Lordship and the authority of His apostles and prophets and at the same time to reject their unequivocal teaching regarding the inspiration and authority of Scripture is not consistent. This inner logic explains the crucial place assumed in church history by the doctrine of Biblical authority.

This issue, it must be added, does not merely concern some single, though important doctrine of Christianity. At stake is the whole orthodox method of building theology. Throughout history the standard of doctrine for all evangelical churches was the Bible. The Bible was the only infallible rule of faith and practice. In its creeds the Church professed a system of doctrine taught in the Bible. The teaching of Scripture was the foundation of orthodox theology.

Modernism rejected that foundation. It sought to build its doctrine first upon a red-letter New Testament, upon the teaching of Jesus alone, later upon Christian experience, and finally upon the unaided human intellect. Biblical truth was to be judged at the bar of human reason. Those parts of Scripture were to be accepted that could be established according to the canons of the science of history, or according to the principles of comparative religious psychology, or according to the systematic coherence of Biblical truths within the framework of some system of human philosophy.

The Neo-orthodox seek to bridge the gap between Modernism and orthodoxy. They seek a foundation ultimately in a mystical intuition which, however, is closely associated with the Bible. The Bible in their thought becomes an authority *in part*. This, however, is to set another foundation for Christian doctrine just as much as did the Modernists of a generation ago. If the Neo-orthodox are successful, then the Christian Church will have to build a new theology upon a new basis, and that new basis is not the teaching of the Bible.

Here lies the crucial difference between the most conservative of the Neo-orthodox and every true evangelical. Genuine evangelical theology is based upon the teaching of the whole Bible received as the authoritative written Word of God. Its theology rests solidly upon the holy Scriptures, for they and they alone are not only able to make us wise unto salvation but are also possessed of God-given authority and are profitable for doctrine. Not a jot or tittle of Scripture can be set aside as void by any true follower of Jesus Christ.

THREE

THE PERSON OF CHRIST

STUART CORNELIUS HACKETT

Dr. Stuart C. Hackett is Professor, and chairman of the department, of Philosophy at Louisiana College, Pineville, Louisiana, where he has been teaching since 1957. Prior to his present appointment he served as Professor of Theology at Western Conservative Baptist Theological Seminary in Portland, Oregon, and later at Conservative Baptist Theological Seminary of Denver, Colorado. An ordained Baptist minister, Dr. Hackett received the A.B. in philosophy from Cornell University, the A.M. in Biblical Literature from Wheaton Graduate School, and the Ph.D. in philosophy from Syracuse University. His book The Resurrection of Theism *(1957) represents his first contribution to that field.*

The Person of Jesus Christ is indisputably the central reality of historic Christian faith. Not only is His Person the very essence of that faith; but every other doctrine of Christian belief comes to its adequate expression only through the understanding of Christ Himself. God, man, sin, redemption, revelation: all these are obscure apart from the climax of Divine Self-Revelation in the Lord Jesus.

If the Person of Christ is thus decisive for essential Christianity, it is our obligation as intelligent men to understand the meaning of Christ as He confronts us in the apostolic witness of the New Testament, which constitutes our bridge of connection with the Christ of history. This witness implies a definite concept of the relation of Jesus Christ to both God and man.

When this witness is expanded and interpreted by historic Christian theology, it confronts us with several basic theological insights. First is the unity of God in His essence: "one God" — the ultimate ground of the existence of the world, the personal Creator beside whom there is no other, the Holy One who providentially directs the whole of His creation toward the fulfilment of His divine purpose.

Another is the eternal trinity of God in His personal being — the existence of this one divine essence in three distinct and separable Persons, Father, Son, and Holy Spirit. These personal distinctions are not temporary, but eternal; not merely aspects of the Divine being, but individual embodiments of that being in its entirety, with mutual personal relations of awareness and fellowship.

A third insight is the unique incarnation of God in the person of Jesus Christ, who is therefore God the Son and yet truly man in such a way that this true deity and true humanity are united and preserved in one single personal self-consciousness.

Finally, this miraculous incarnation was accomplished historically through the work of the Holy Spirit in such a way that Jesus Christ derived His whole humanity from His mother Mary, entirely apart from the instrumentality of a male parent.

These summary affirmations represent, as do all the great creedal confessions of mainline Christianity, the attempt to express the indispensable intellectual aspects of Christian conviction concerning Jesus Christ. The original point of departure for all such confessions was (and is) the historical reality of God in Jesus Christ Himself. Since, however, between this reality and every Christian generation except the first, there has stood the definitive New Testament (and ultimately the whole Biblical witness to Christ), the point of departure becomes secondarily but indispensably that very Biblical witness itself.

THE ESSENTIAL NEW TESTAMENT WITNESS TO CHRIST

If then we approach the New Testament in its entirety as we have it, we find that while there are varying degrees of emphasis and differing levels of explicit assertion, there still remains what may be called an organic unity of Christological affirmation. This Christological affirmation involves precisely those convictions that we have already had occasion to mention: that Jesus Christ was a human being; that He was at the same time one with the Father in deity, though subordinated to the Father in some sense not inconsistent with this deity; and that He was for all that a single person with a single self-consciousness. It is not the case, of course, that these insights are mechanically and monotonously repeated in the various layers of New Testament literature; there are more explicit references along with veiled implications. But directly or indirectly the implications are there in all the levels of the literature. There are easily accessible any number of works which summarize the evidence for this conclusion: two of the best being those of Mackintosh [1] and B. B. Warfield.[2] For our purpose, it will be sufficient to cite samples of this united testimony; and since the reality of Christ's humanity is not seriously in dispute on the contemporary scene, we shall be principally occupied with the New Testament witness to Christ's deity.

At the outset, the New Testament lends no support to the idea that the union of deity and humanity in Christ was only a moral unity which did not involve a single personal self-consciousness. It is one and the same Christ Jesus who in His wealth assumes the poverty of human existence that we might thereby become rich (2 Cor. 8:9); it is the one man Christ Jesus who is the Mediator (I Tim. 2:5); it is the same person who empties Himself in becoming man that He might endure the death of the cross (Phil. 2:5–8); it is the true Logos of life that was manifested for human hands to feel (I John 1:1). In the Gospels Jesus always appears as a single self-conscious person, a single *I*. As theologians frequently observe, the Logos is not separate from the man Jesus, nor is the man Jesus separate from the Logos. While Jesus frequently speaks of His unity with the Father (which therefore implies personal distinctness), He never says, "I and the Logos are one." Any consideration which involved a duality of personal principles in Jesus Christ would therefore run counter to the whole grain of New Testament belief.

As for the witness to the deity of Christ, we find this implication concerning the ultimate significance of Christ's person in every section of the New Testament, though not always with the same degree of explicit doctrinal assertion. As a matter of fact, the incidental way in which reference to the Godhead of Christ occurs is itself strong evidence that a supernatural view of Christ was the common and accepted belief of those for whose needs the New Testament books were originally penned. In considering the various levels of New Testament literature, we may distinguish the following principal literary groups, arranged approximately in the order of their chronological origin: the Pauline literature, the Synoptic Gospels and Acts (possibly also First Peter), the rest of the General Epistles except the Johannine, Hebrews, the Apocalypse, and the Johannine Gospel and letters.

One or two words of caution are appropriate here. First, no critical implications about authorship should be drawn from this list: it is, for example, entirely possible that the Apocalypse and the Johannine literature were produced by the same writer. Again, these literary groups may (as critical analysis and historical insight suggest) lead us back to earlier traditions whose order is not necessarily suggested by the chronological order in which the books themselves were written. The Gospels, for example, while written *after* many of Paul's epistles, represent traditions which historically antedate the Pauline theology. In any case, the significant point is that every layer of New Testament literature embodies a high Christology from which purely humanitarian views of Christ are entirely absent; the whole presents a supernatural Christ.

Paul presents a supernatural Christ in the very earliest stratum of his works. He asserts the deity of Christ in the highest possible terms by stating that Christ Jesus possessed the essential form of deity and a complex equality with God (Phil. 2:6). Paul declares that in Christ there dwells all the fulness of the Godhead in its entirety (Col. 2:9). He calls Christ "the God who is over all, blessed forever" (Rom. 9:5); and Paul speaks of "our great God and Saviour, Jesus Christ" (Titus 2:13). It is worth noting, moreover, that in all of these passages the Christological inference is incidental to the argument so that it must have been common ground between Paul and the Christians to whom he wrote.

The Synoptic Gospels and Acts, together with First Peter,

confront us with the same implication. The Christ of the Gospel of Mark, for example, is no mere prophetic teacher but the supernatural Son of God (3:11, 5:7, 15:39) and the Messianic Son of Man. (See especially Mark 8:29-31 and note the interchange of the titles of Messiah and Son of Man.) The Markan Jesus not only claims to be the Messiah of the Old Testament anticipation, but He interprets His messiahship in the highest terms. He admits (14:61) to the high priest that He is the Messiah, the Son of the Blessed One, and He specifically refers to the 110th Psalm as showing that the Messiah is not merely David's son but David's Lord (12:35-37). This last passage not only is unintelligible unless Jesus refers to Himself therein, but it makes clear that Jesus interpreted His messiahship in the sense of divine Lordship. If in turn we find that the Old Testament asserts elsewhere (as in Isaiah 9:6, 7) the absolute deity of the Messiah, who can deny that Jesus specifically applied this implication to his messiahship? That the writer himself held the highest view of Christ is further evident from the fact that at the outset of his Gospel he depicts John the Baptist as the forerunner of Jesus Christ and describes this in the words of Isaiah as a preparation of the way of the Lord Himself (1:2, 3).

The testimony of the other two synoptic Gospels is equally clear. The Markan witness is reinforced even more explicitly. Matthew cites the promise of Christ to be in the midst of His disciples wherever two or three of them are gathered together (18:20). He tells how the risen Christ assured His followers that He would be with them always (28:20), and how He commanded them to baptize into *the* name of the Father and of the Son and of the Holy Spirit (28:19). He asserts Jesus' claim, as Son of Man, to possess the divine prerogative of the forgiveness of sins (6:14, 15;

9:2, 6); and to be the final judge of the destinies of all men (25:31–46). That all of these assertions are explicable only as implying deity seems apparent.

The impact of Luke's witness both in his Gospel and in Acts is precisely to the same effect. In the Gospel, the messiahship of Christ is abundantly asserted (2:11, 2:26, 4:41, 9:20, 20:41, 22:67, 23:2, 24:26, 46, etc.); and it is clear that this title involves the full orb of meaning that we have already noted in Mark. As in the other Synoptics, the title "Son of Man" again carries its full weight. Here too Jesus is the forgiver of sins (5:24), the one to be seated at the right hand of God's power (22:69), and the determiner of the final destinies of men (9:26, 12:8, 21:36). In Acts, the situation is no different. Jesus is addressed in prayer (7:59), is referred to as "Lord over all" (10:36), and is continually mentioned by the title "Lord" in such a way as to express "the highest conceivable exaltation and authority on the part of Jesus Himself." The representation of Paul in Acts 20:28, speaking of the "church of God, which He purchased with His own blood," implies the highest possible Christology: the absolute Godhead of the Saviour.

First Peter implies likewise a high Christology. It was the very Spirit of Christ that testified through the Old Testament prophets (1:11); angels and authorities are subject to Christ (3:22); and believers are to "sanctify in your hearts Christ Jesus as Lord" (3:15) — a passage which recalls Isaiah 8:13 which specifically refers to Jehovah. Here is no studied Christological dogma; but the supernatural Christ is obviously in full view.

The same witness appears in the General Epistles, in Hebrews, and finally in the Apocalypse. Peter speaks of "our God and Saviour, Jesus Christ" (2 Peter 1:1). James mentions "the Name," obviously referring to Jesus and thus applying to Him an Old Testament designation of Jehovah (James 5:14). He speaks also of Christ as "the Glory" in a way reminiscent of the same title applied to Jehovah in Zechariah 2:5 (James 2:1). The writer of Hebrews depicts Christ as the One to whom God was speaking in Psalm 45:6 when He said, "Thy throne, O God, is forever and ever" (Hebrews 1:8), and as the Lord who created the world (Hebrews 1:10). Finally, we read of Jesus as being with God, the first and the last (Rev. 21:6; 1:8, 17, 18; 22:13), as well as the object of worship and adoration (Rev. 5:13, 7:10; 21:22, 23). This last passage (21:22, 23) parallels Isaiah 60:19 and implies the oneness of Christ with God in the highest sense. The impact of these combined insights indicates a basic unity of Christological affirmation — an affirmation which understands Jesus Christ as one in being with God.

The Johannine witness to Christ's Godhead is so full and abundant that a passing recognition is sufficient. The prologue of the Gospel specifically identifies the Word who became flesh as God (1:1, 14). Jesus Himself declares His oneness with the Father (10:30, 14:9) and He appropriates to Himself the Old Testament designation of Jehovah as the "I am" (8:58). One of the climaxes of the theme of the Gospel comes in the affirmation of Thomas that Jesus, as risen, is "My Lord and my God" (20:28). In the First Epistle, moreover, it is declared that "we are in Him that is true, in his Son Jesus Christ. This one is the true God and eternal life" (I John 5:20). It is difficult to imagine how a clearer designation of Christ's Godhead could be affirmed than is indicated by these Johannine assertions.

The essential New Testament witness to the deity of Christ is therefore clear. Taking the various layers of literature as they lie at hand in their present form, it is impossible to avoid the conclusion that the uniform New Testament witness affirms the supernatural being and, ultimately, the Godhead of Jesus Christ. A careful analysis of these layers will further conclude that the witness to Christ's deity ultimately rests upon the self-testimony of the Lord Jesus Christ as He confronted the apostolic circle from which the New Testament witness originated. Any attempt, therefore, to bypass the united Biblical witness must ultimately result in an attack on the character of Christ Himself.

Now if the claim to deity does revert to Jesus, what does this imply for the doctrine of Christology? Christian minds have elaborated the answer in unnumbered ways. If Jesus did announce this claim, and if Jesus is the person of humility, love, and self-giving described in the Gospels, and if Jesus is the person through whom the Christian Church came into existence, and if Jesus is a person of unimpeachable honesty; and if, finally, this same Jesus is the person whose Spirit has transformed uncounted souls through the centuries of Christian history, then it seems that the only satisfactory explanation of His claim is the recognition of the truth that in Christ we actually confront God in history.

The claim to deity on the other hand, can be made falsely. As Warfield puts it:

We are not absurdly arguing that the claim to be God is one which cannot be made by a human being untruly . . . But why should we absurdly argue that Jesus may be supposed to have done whatever we think within the compass of human folly or human wickedness? . . . Neither Jesus nor His followers could have invented the claims to deity which Jesus is reported to have made for Himself: for the truth of these claims is needed to account both for Jesus and for His followers.[3]

In a former day, when hostile criticism was dominant, the universal assumption of classical liberalism was that, whatever else He might be, Jesus was not literally and personally God. Instead, He was the highest embodiment of the human potential for God-consciousness, or the champion of God's ethical kingdom, or the historical symbol of the oneness of humanity with the Divine Being. Thus could Schleiermacher, Ritschl, and Hegel elaborate the meaning of Jesus for their contemporaries. The first of these thinkers may be cited as an example of such a liberal outlook.

For Friedrich Schleiermacher, Christ is that historical person who in all His life realized the highest human potential for God-consciousness. In whatever sense He was "divine" it was not a sense which made Him, in His person, different in kind from other human beings; the difference was one of degree only. To be sure, Christ is in a sense unique as the full historical realization of this latent human possibility; and it is through Him that the rest of us can move in the direction of a comparable though relative realization. Schleiermacher sums it up as follows: "If Christ be placed at the summit, as the individual who was entirely pervaded by the God-consciousness, and therefore taken up into full unity with the Highest, everywhere else there exists only an imperfect and unequal pervasion, which decreases steadily within the sphere of rational being. . . ." [4] For such a theology, then, Christ is not the essence of revelation, the Word which is God Himself. He is merely the highest example of the divine potential in human existence.

This belief in a purely human Jesus, however highly He may have realized the human potential, is unsupported by historical analysis. The only evidence for it is the indisputable fact that the Christ of the Gospel history is fully and completely human. Not only, however, is this assertion part and parcel of orthodox Christology itself, but the attempt to push the real humanity to mere humanity has, ultimately, only the support of a subjective philosophical preference, which makes an incarnation impossible by definition. In any case, contemporary Christology includes a vigorous segment of thought which repudiates this purely humanitarian Christology and reasserts a truly divine Christ.

REASSERTION OF THE UNIQUE DIVINE CHRIST: ESSENTIAL REVELATION

The reinstatement of traditional Christology is characteristic of two streams in contemporary theological thought. On the one hand, there is the continuing and growing tradition of a thoroughly orthodox theology itself, of which B. B. Warfield, Hermann Bavinck, and G. C. Berkouwer may be taken as fairly typical Protestant representatives. On the other hand, there is the rapidly expanding right wing of the so-called new orthodoxy represented by Karl Barth and Emil Brunner.

To this second stream of thought we wish to direct our passing attention. Here we find a strong traditionalism in Christology in company with the most radical conclusions about literary New Testament criticism, which reject infallible Biblical authority. In any case, it is indisputable that Barth and Brunner believe in the absolute deity of Jesus Christ as the Word who is God in history. In fact, it is just because Jesus *is* God the Word that He is also the very essence of divine revelation in its objective aspect. Thus Barth affirms: "The Reality of which we are now speaking, God's revelation in Jesus Christ, is compelling and exclusive . . . because here we have not to do with a reality different from God, but with God Himself, with God in the highest, with the Creator of Heaven and earth . . ." [5] Barth makes it clear in the whole of his first volume of *Church Dogmatics* that this ascription is to be understood in the context of the church doctrine of the Trinity, so that Jesus Christ "does not first become God's Son or Word in the event of revelation . . . Jesus Christ reveals Himself as the person he already is antecedently, even apart from this event, actually in himself." [6]

Brunner's affirmation is to the same effect. He clearly expresses his repudiation of the classical liberal Christology by declaring that "the most enthusiastic panegyric about Jesus" does not indicate even the "faintest spark of real faith in Christ" so long as the speaker confines Christ to the sphere of humanity.[7] When we consider Christ, "there is no idea of a *primus inter pares* (first among equals), but of one who is essentially the only One . . . because in principle He is different from us, who are creatures." [8] Jesus indeed possesses the divine nature which means "that which is related to God — as God Himself." [9] And this specifically implies the orthodox doctrine of the "Two Natures," the doctrine of Chalcedon.[10] As with Barth, Brunner's belief involves traditional Trinitarianism.[11] He advocates a full Christology which includes the impersonal humanity of Christ in such a way that at the point where man has sinful personality, Jesus "has, or rather is, the divine person of the Logos." [12]

There are perhaps in the Christology of these thinkers, secondary assertions which do not quite measure up to form. Brunner, for example, while asserting that the incarnation of God in Christ is a saving miracle, cannot believe that this requires belief in the virgin birth of Christ, though he thinks it better to be thoroughly orthodox here than to overthrow the whole content of the unique revelation of God in Christ.[13] Barth, for his part, thinks of Christ as assuming human nature "under the presupposition of the Fall" (i.e. human nature guilty before God), yet in such a way that Christ does not actually sin.[14] But while these shortcomings may detract from the outward radiance, they in no sense destroy the central brilliance of the clear Christological light that is given. Here, at least, is a vibrant faith in Christ — the Christ of traditional orthodoxy and of history.

It is by no means the case that the "liberal Christ" has disappeared from the contemporary scene, though He be hidden in new theological phrases. Thus John Knox can speak of the "Divine Nature" of Christ, and then go on to explain that this representation is not metaphysically accurate but a symbolic reference to God's saving act through the human Jesus, so that "God's action *is* the divine nature of Christ." [15] Again, D. M. Baillie can entitle his greatest book *God Was in Christ* and then proceed to dissolve this very affirmation for all practical purposes. For him, Jesus was in every sense a human person with a human self-consciousness, while at the same time He was the incarnation of the divine Word. This is not the revival of an ancient heresy; it is instead a paradox.[16] Despite this claim, however, such a paradox leaves us no real incarnation, but merely a combination of the Logos with the separately personal and human Jesus. Baillie does not leave the paradox there, however. He attempts to understand it in terms of the general paradox of God's grace: God was incarnate in Jesus in the sense that the latter lived His whole life in conscious recognition that all was done in total dependence upon God's grace.[17] "Jesus Christ is the One in whom human selfhood fully came to its own and lived its fullest life . . . because His human selfhood was wholly yielded to God." [18] But here, there is no genuine being of God *personally* in Jesus Christ; and therefore, under cover of the "most enthusiastic panegyric," the liberal Jesus reappears, somewhat elevated, but nevertheless His old self.

In Paul Tillich, finally, the liberal Jesus, the Jesus of mythical symbolism, steps forth in bold relief. He writes, "The assertion that Jesus as the Christ is the personal unity of a divine and a human nature must be replaced by the assertion that in Jesus as the Christ the eternal unity of God and man has become historical reality." [19] In all these liberal survivals, the Christ of classic liberalism emerges again, though in the garb of a more exalted phraseology. There is therefore no alternative but to strip it of its external garb and pronounce it twice dead. If the argument in principle buries the Christology of Schleiermacher, it carries all its successors into the same grave.

Since there appears to be a revival of a genuine Christology in right wing neo-orthodoxy, we must at the same time ask whether this revival has fully felt the impact of a position which ascribes absolute deity, absolute personal and conscious identity with God, to the historical Jesus. What are the implications of this ascription for a relevant Biblical apologetic in the defense of Christian truth? On this question we may be only suggestive, but we dare not be silent!

CHRISTOLOGY THE CENTRAL BASIS FOR AN APOLOGETIC OF SPECIAL REVELATION

Traditional Christological witness is inexplicable apart from its truth. If Jesus Himself, not to mention His Church, cannot be explained unless He is God in history, He provides the central evidence of a Christian theistic philosophy which asserts that the ultimate Ground of existence, the Absolute Creator, has intervened in history by appearing personally in the context of human life.

If Jesus Christ is God in history, then this same Eternal Word put His stamp of approval on the written word of Scripture as possessing infallible authority.[20] He promised to His disciples the influence of His Spirit, the Spirit of Truth, in guiding them into all truth (Jn. 14:26, 16:13–15; cf. also Luke 24:48, 49). On this basis the spiritual authority of Scripture may be regarded as absolute and as supported by God the Word in history.

A C. H. Dodd may boggle at such a conclusion, implying as it does the identity of Scripture with the word of God written. We may reply that the sole support for Dodd's objection is the assumption that we can accept as authoritative only those words ascribed to Jesus which commend themselves to our moral judgment and conscience as worthy.[21] The relative subjectivism of such a criterion is obvious: a judgment of moral worth which occupies a position above that of the Gospels will do well to examine its own foundations. Of neo-orthodoxy we must therefore ask the question whether its rejection of objective Biblical revelation is compatible with its vigorous affirmation that Jesus Christ is precisely the revelation of God, because He is God the Word in history.

The doctrine of the person of Christ is therefore a firm foundation for an apologetic of special divine revelation. This apologetic carries with it the spiritual authority of written Scripture as the very word of God. Important as this is, however, it must not divert us from the main conclusion of our whole argument. In the Christ of the New

Testament we confront the Jesus of history who is God Himself entering history and human life for our salvation. In such a conclusion we do not merely rest; instead, we kneel to seek that salvation and to offer the sacrifice of thanksgiving that ascends to God from the innermost being of the redeemed soul.

FOUR

REDEMPTION BY CHRIST

T. LEONARD LEWIS

Dr. Lewis was graduated from Wheaton College (Ph.B.) in 1931. He received his theological education from Northern Baptist Seminary, where he took the B.D. degree and the Th.D. He was ordained to the ministry in 1928, and held the pastorate of the Harrison Avenue Baptist Church in Oak Park, Illinois, from 1929 to 1941; was Professor of Theology at Northern Baptist Seminary (1941–44), and was elected President at Gordon College in 1944. He died suddenly in March 1959, before this volume went to press.

The need for some power that can check the destructive tendencies of man and that can heal the wounds which he has inflicted on himself is desperate. Through many avenues of reform he has consistently sought to remove the evils that have plagued him and to improve his lot morally and socially. Such effort, however, has not availed much. He has more legislation, and less observance of the spirit of law. He has more checks on economic failure, and less certainty for the economic future. If the present moral conditions of American civilization are any index of the general trend throughout the world, he has not advanced far beyond the attainments of the Roman Empire. The grave question facing human society is not what it will be like a century from now, but whether it will survive at all. If it does survive, will its character be worth perpetuating?

Many religions have sought to regulate or to discipline the life of man by holding before him ethical standards which he should follow in order to realize the highest values. They have failed to produce a dynamic whereby he can achieve them. Obviously some power is needed that will enable him to escape from the consequences of his evil deeds, and that will lift him to new heights.

Contemporary thinkers lay great emphasis on the redemption of society. Inasmuch as society is constituted of individuals, it becomes apparent that it cannot be redeemed apart from the redemption of individuals. Redemption by Christ is the theme of the whole Bible, for as the late Dr. James M. Gray used to say in lectures to his students, "The Bible is a history of the redemption of the human race upon this earth."

In the early accounts of Jesus' birth, redemption was given a prominent place. Simeon, beholding the child Jesus and knowing that he looked upon the Lord's Christ, said, "Lord, now lettest thou thy servant depart in peace, according to thy word: for mine eyes have seen thy salvation, which thou hast prepared before the face of all people; a light to lighten the Gentiles, and the glory of thy people Israel (Lk. 2:29–32). Anna, a prophetess, entering the temple and hearing Simeon, gave evidence also that she knew Jesus as the redeemer as she "gave thanks likewise unto the Lord, and spake of him to all them that looked for redemption in Jerusalem" (Lk. 2:38).

When Jesus began His public ministry, He was identified

by John the Baptist: "Behold the Lamb of God, which taketh away the sin of the world" (John 1:29). Our Lord's redemptive purpose in His life and death was proved by His own words: "For the Son of man came not to be ministered unto, but to minister, and to give his life a ransom for many" (Mk. 10:45).

Redemption by Christ is both objective and subjective. What He did *for us* on the cross, He desires to do *in us* by His Holy Spirit. On the cross He died as the substitute for our sins; by His victory over death and the grave, and by His ascension and the gift of the Holy Spirit, the subjective work of Christ in us is made possible.

Redemption carries with it two basic ideas: ransom from sin's condemnation and guilt, and deliverance by power from sin's bondage and corruption. In the record of the first Passover (Exod. 12) both ideas are clearly seen. The blood of the Passover lamb was shed and applied, and the power of God was exhibited in delivering the people of Israel from the bondage in Egypt. So in the New Testament, believers are saved from the penalty of sin by Christ's death, and are delivered from the power and dominion of sin by the benefits of His atoning death. These benefits of our Lord's redemptive work, union with Christ, regeneration, conversion, justification and adoption, sanctification and glorification, are applied to believers by the Holy Spirit. Thus, what our Lord begins in us He will bring to fruition in the day of Jesus Christ (Phil. 1:6).

The vocabulary describing redemption in the New Testament illustrates its various aspects. A word used only once (*peripoieo*) is translated "purchased" in Acts 20:28: "Take heed unto yourselves, and to all the flock, over the which the Holy Ghost hath made you overseers, to feed the church of God, which he hath purchased with his own blood." Christ gained possession of the church by the purchase price of His own blood.

Another word often used in either verb or noun form denotes the payment of a ransom price, substitutionary in character: (*lutroo, lutron, apolutrosis*). "[He] gave himself for us that he might redeem us from all iniquity" (Titus 2:14). The idea is that of a ransom price, paid as a substitution in order to free the objects of redemption. Again, "Ye know that ye were not redeemed with corruptible things as silver and gold . . . but with the precious blood of Christ, as of a lamb without blemish and without spot" (I Pet. 1:18, 19). In this passage the sacrifice of Christ is contrasted with redemption by silver or gold. The blood of Christ is the payment made to obtain "eternal redemption" (Heb. 9:12), for those that were under the first covenant (Heb. 9:15). "Redemption that is in Christ Jesus" is also the ground of justification (Romans 3:24).

A third word (*agoradzo*) simply means "to buy." The *agora* was the bazaar, or the market place. The verb originally meant *to buy in the market place*. Paul used this word purposefully when he wrote to the Corinthians: "Know ye not that . . . ye are not your own? For ye are bought with a price . . ." (I Cor. 6:19, 20). The triumphant redeemed in heaven sing: "Thou wast slain, and hast redeemed us to God by thy blood out of every kindred, and tongue, and people, and nation; and hast made us unto our God kings and priests: and we shall reign on the earth" (Rev. 5:9, 10).

In the first Christian century, the word "redemption" signified to the Greeks the purchase price for the freedom of a slave. In America before the Civil War men of good will and of means frequently attended the auctions of slaves in the South. Having outbid other prospective buyers, they paid the price demanded for the slave, not to continue his enslavement but to set him free. All this the Lord does by His redemption.

The substitutionary work of the Lord Jesus Christ is beautifully portrayed in the five Levitical offerings (Lev. 1-7). Whereas they are described in order as the burnt offering, the meal (*meat* — KJV) offering, the peace offering, the sin offering, and the trespass offering, the order of our experience of need of a Saviour is in reverse. Our first need is for a Saviour who can expiate our trespasses. The sense of having committed an act of transgression produces a feeling of guilt. The Lord Jesus is presented in the New Testament as the trespass offering: "He bare our sins in his own body on the tree" (I Pet. 2:24), and through His atonement our guilt is removed.

The individual transgression, expiated by the trespass offering, is not, however, the cause of sin but the result of sin. The deed done is simply the proof that one is a sinner by nature. The trespass is the fruit of which the sin in our nature is the root. A further look at Calvary reveals that on the cross our Lord "who knew no sin was made *sin* [a sin-offering] for us, that we might be made the righteousness of God in him" (II Cor. 5:21).

Reconcilation with God follows the removal of sin. The believer appropriates the Lord Jesus as his peace offering: "Therefore, being justified by faith, we have peace with God through our Lord Jesus Christ" (Rom. 5:1). He ". . . made peace through the blood of his cross" (Col. 1:20).

The fourth offering is the meal (meat) offering of fine flour and oil, which represents the perfection of the Lord Jesus as a man. There was no unevenness in His character, no lack of balance in His personality. Since God asks for perfection from imperfect human beings, it is comforting to know that the Lord Jesus is the meal offering, the perfect One presented on our behalf.

The whole burnt offering speaks of the complete consecration of the victim to God. It is a picture of the perfect obedience which is due Him, the entire dedication of personality, time, talents, and energy. We cannot understand the meaning of consecration until we are born-again Christians and have begun to grow in grace. We realize what we owe to God, but we know, too, that we come short of doing what we ought. It is wonderful then, to hear the Lord Jesus Christ as our whole burnt offering saying: "I come to do thy will, O God" (Heb. 10:7), and to know that, while perfectly doing the Father's will in complete dedication to the Father's glory, He is our whole burnt offering. "Jesus paid it all!"

Union with Christ, while not a Biblical phrase, describes the basis for Christian living. Jesus stated it in germ in John 14:20: "At that day ye shall know that I am in my Father, and ye in me, and I in you." The last seven words of the verse are of particular significance: "Ye in me, and I in you." "Ye in me" refers to our position in Christ; "I in you," to His dwelling in us. Both are true in the Christian's experience. When one becomes a Christian by faith in Jesus Christ as Lord and Saviour, he moves out of an old life outside of Christ into a new life "in Christ." Dr. Adolf Deissmann stated that the Apostle Paul used the expression "in Christ" or its equivalent 164 times in his epistles referring to the sphere of the believer's life and blessings.

Union with Christ is possible because of the identification of our Lord Jesus Christ with our humanity. The author of Hebrews wrote, "Forasmuch as the children are partakers of flesh and blood, he also himself likewise took part of the same . . ." (Heb. 2:14). Paul wrote concerning Christ:

"Who being in the form of God thought it not robbery to be equal with God: but made himself of no reputation, and took upon him the form of a servant, and was made in the likeness of men" (Phil. 2:6, 7), and Matthew declared concerning the birth of Jesus: "Now all this was done that it might be fulfilled which was spoken of the Lord by the prophet, saying, Behold, a virgin shall be with child, and shall bring forth a son, and they shall call his name Emanuel, which being interpreted is, God with us" (Matt. 1:22, 23). The incarnation of God the Son as Jesus of Nazareth, both God and man, was necessary to make possible the union of believers with Christ. Jesus Christ lived among men a perfect life in obedience to the Father, that He might enter into the lives of those who received Him as Saviour and Lord.

Robert William Dale wrote that Jesus is different from any other man who ever lived, for He is the kind of Person who will walk right out of the pages of the New Testament and into the lives of those who receive Him by faith. "But as many as received him, to them he gave the right to become the children of God, even to them that believe on his name" (John 1:12 ARV).

The epistles of Paul teach that, being united to Christ by the work of the Holy Spirit in response to faith, the believer is involved in crucifixion, death, burial, quickening, and resurrection with Christ. After his conversion, Paul came to understand that a union had been effected between Christ and himself, so that he could say, "I am crucified with Christ, nevertheless I live; yet not I, but Christ liveth in me: and the life I now live in the flesh I live by the faith of the Son of God, who loved me, and gave himself for me" (Gal. 2:20). This is the secret of a successful, holy Christian life.

Believers are not only crucified and dead with Christ,

but are risen with Him (Col. 3:1), to walk in newness of life. The new life is the power of His resurrection based upon union with Him. A Great Lakes steamer proceeding from Lake Huron through St. Mary's River and into the locks at the Soo is lifted by the water of Lake Superior from the low level of St. Mary's River to the upper level of the lake, 22 feet higher, and then moves out upon that upper level. Similarly, the saving grace of God having united us to Christ, enables us to live on the upper level of fellowship with Him.

This union with Christ guarantees power adequate to live the Christian life victoriously, so that every believer may say with the Apostle Paul: "I can do all things through Christ which strengtheneth me" (Phil. 4:13). This strengthening is not from without but from within; for Paul literally wrote: "I can do all things through Christ who (in)strengtheneth me," because "Christ liveth in me." Other results of this union with Christ are fellowship with the risen Lord, ultimate conformity to His image and likeness, and security for all eternity. Paul voiced his sense of obligation for these blessings by saying: "For to me to live is Christ and to die is gain" (Phil. 1:21).

In the salvation which Christ bestows upon believers, the first act of God following conviction by the Holy Spirit is that of regeneration. Logically, not chronologically, union with Christ precedes regeneration. Chronologically, union with Christ, regeneration, and conversion are simultaneous. "Regeneration," to quote Augustus Hopkins Strong, "is that act of God by which the governing disposition of the soul is made holy, and by which, through the truth as a means, the first holy exercise of this disposition is secured." [1] The great words used by Paul are "justification" and "righteousness," but John's words are "birth" and "life." Jesus said to

Nicodemus, "Except a man be born again, he cannot see the kingdom of God" (John 3:3). He explained why the new birth is necessary: "That which is born of the flesh is flesh; and that which is born of the Spirit is spirit" (John 3:6). The first birth which constitutes us members of the human family is of the flesh. From physical birth we receive the nature of the flesh which is self-centered and sinful. The natural bent of man's disposition is inherited from Adam, whose sin brought death and produced the disposition toward evil which is called depravity. No matter what one does to the flesh, it remains flesh. It can be educated, cultured, refined, and even religious, as in the case of Nicodemus, but it is always, ever, and only flesh, and "that which is born of the flesh is flesh." The new birth is absolutely necessary.

The Old Testament Scriptures had promised a better day when God would do an internal work in the hearts of men and lives would be changed: "A new heart also will I give you, and a new spirit will I put within you: and I will take away the stony heart out of your flesh, and I will give you a heart of flesh" (Ezek. 36:26). Jeremiah also had given a word of promise: "After those days, saith the Lord, I will put my law in their inward parts, and write it in their hearts . . ." (Jer. 31:33). Those promises concerned God's actions in changing the governing dispositions of the soul. Jeremiah's word of encouragement was connected with the promised New Covenant which the Lord introduced at the Last Supper the night before His crucifixion. The Old Covenant, the Ten Commandments, had been written on tables of stone, but the New Covenant was to be written in the hearts of men. The change promised was not to be the result of human effort or of the human will, but a birth from God: "But as many as received him, to them he gave the right to become the children of God, even to them that believe on his name: who were born, not of blood, nor of the will of the flesh, nor of the will of man, but of God" (John 1:12, 13 ARV).

The change brought about in the life by the new birth is a change of desire, disposition, and appetite: "If any man be in Christ, he is a new creature; old things are passed away; behold, all things are become new" (II Cor. 5:17). A noted evangelist, accustomed to holding city-wide and county-wide campaigns in the South, was persuaded to stump the South in the interests of prohibition. He later declared that he was not aware that any saloons had been closed as a result of his prohibition lectures; but he recalled that in the days of his greatest evangelistic ministry, towns, cities, and counties had gone dry as a result of the preaching of the gospel and the changed lives of the converts. It may be helpful to remove the means of gratifying an appetite, but it is far better to remove the appetite itself.

The new birth is not a process but a crisis. There may have been many preparatory factors leading up to the new birth, but the new birth itself is instantaneous. In the good providence of God, circumstances, events, crises, counsel from friends or pastor, sickness, or a combination of factors may have contributed toward preparation for the new birth. The new birth itself is an act of God wrought deep within the soul, below the conscious level, and is known only by its results. At the instant of birth an infant is not aware of having been born into the human family, but as a result of the birth it begins at once to breathe, cries, and is soon giving evidence of hunger. Just so the new birth results in life, a cry, and hunger for the food of God's Word, thus demonstrating that a spiritual birth has taken place. This change is not something apart from Christ, but is the result of union with Him.

Regeneration is the work of the Holy Spirit using the Word of God as an instrument. Reformers like Luther and Calvin gave little place in their writings to the doctrine of the new birth, but the subject came into prominence during the revivals under John Wesley, who emphasized the truth that the Holy Spirit uses the Word of God to bring about the new birth. The Word of God is truth, but the soul needs something to be done in it to enable it to comprehend the truth, just as a blind man needs something more than light in order that he may see. When sight is restored, then the light can be appreciated. James writes: "Of his own will begat he us with the word of truth" (Jas. 1:18), and Peter wrote: "Being born again, not of corruptible seed, but of incorruptible, by the Word of God which liveth and abideth forever" (I Pet. 1:23). The Holy Spirit illuminates the mind and prompts the appropriation of the truth.

In the change that results, there is the incoming of a new life principle: "Christ liveth in me" (Gal. 2:20); "He that hath the Son hath life" (I John 5:12). Thus, in regeneration, believers become partakers of the divine nature (II Pet. 1:4), and the recipients of the eternal life of God through Jesus Christ, a quality of life that is not present in the unregenerate. The evidences of regeneration are not the memory of a past experience of grace years ago but a present inward love for Jesus Christ, His people, His work in the world, and His Word. Conversion and sanctification are the best proofs that the new birth has taken place in any life.

Jesus said: "Except ye be converted, and become as little children, ye shall not enter into the kingdom of heaven"

(Matt. 18:3). Conversion, to quote Strong again, "is that voluntary change in the mind of the sinner, in which he turns, on the one hand, from sin, and on the other hand, to Christ." [2] Turning from sin is designated "repentance" and turning to Christ is called "faith." Paul declared to the Ephesian elders that he had preached to Jews and Greeks "repentance toward God, and faith toward our Lord Jesus Christ" (Acts 20:21). Conversion is the human side of the spiritual change which, from the divine side, we call regeneration. While it is true that God turns men to Himself, man is exhorted to turn to God. Our Lord told the paralytic to rise, take up his bed, and walk. It was the man's duty to obey; it was the Lord's delight to enable him to do so (Mark 2:11, 12).

Repentance, the negative aspect of conversion "is that voluntary change in the mind of the sinner in which he turns from sin." [3] The intellect, the emotions, and the will are all involved. The mind recognizes that sin involves personal guilt and defilement: "by the law is the knowledge of sin" (Rom. 3:20). The emotion is effected by the recognition that sin is a transgression against God and, consequently, there is a change of feeling. There is also, however, the volitional element in repentance, a change of purpose, the abandonment of sin.

Job illustrates well the nature of repentance: "I have heard of thee by the hearing of the ear: but now mine eye seeth thee. Wherefore, I abhor myself, and repent in dust and ashes" (Job 42:5, 6). Isaiah experienced the same sort of crisis: "Woe is me! for I am undone; because I am a man of unclean lips, and I dwell in the midst of a people of unclean lips: for mine eyes have seen the King, the Lord of hosts" (Isa. 6:5). Peter cried in distress: "Depart from me; for I am a sinful man, O Lord" (Lk. 5:8). Paul made his confession: "This is a faithful saying, and worthy of all acceptation, that Christ Jesus came into the world to save sinners; of whom I am chief" (I Tim. 1:15). Repentance is not a positive means of salvation; it is only a negative condition. True repentance never exists apart from saving faith. Judas was filled with remorse for his wrong deed and committed suicide. Peter truly repented of denying his Lord and became a useful servant of Christ. Wherever there is true faith, there is true repentance.

Faith is that voluntary change in the mind of the sinner by which he turns to Christ. Like repentance, it is made up of an intellectual, an emotional, and a volitional element. The intellectual element, an historical acceptance of the facts of Scripture and an intellectual belief in man's sinfulness and our Lord's ability to save, is a necessary part; but it is not sufficient for salvation. The emotional element, having the feelings moved by the love of Christ for sinners is also a vital part of faith, but is not sufficient. The volitional element — trust in Jesus Christ as Lord and Saviour, the reception into one's life of the living Lord, and the appropriation of Christ — is necessary to become a Christian (John 1:12). Faith of itself cannot save, but it is the instrument by which Christ and His salvation are received. It does not take a great faith to make one a Christian, but faith in a great Saviour.

Martin Luther rightly is credited with restoring to the church the Biblical truth of justification by faith alone, apart from religious works of any kind. He was raised up at the precise moment of history when his message would be received and understood. Justification is one of the great doctrines of redemption. It is defined as that judicial act of God whereby He declares to be righteous the person who trusts Jesus Christ as Saviour and Lord. It is not something that God does *in* the person who trusts Jesus Christ as Lord, but it is something that He does *for* him. Justification is based upon the Saviour's death as a substitute for sinners and is made effective by the union of the believer with Christ.

The Epistle to the Romans expounds the doctrine of the righteousness of God, showing first that righteousness is reckoned to the account of the sinner who trusts Jesus Christ as Saviour, and then, that righteousness is imparted to him so that he becomes righteous in character as well as in standing. The word translated "justify" uniformly means "to declare righteous," never "to make righteous." In Deuteronomy 25:1 judges were instructed "to justify the righteous and condemn the wicked." That is the correct procedure according to the concept of justice. The New Testament, however, introduces a new principle: "To him that worketh not, but believeth on him that justifieth the ungodly, his faith is counted unto him for righteousness" (Rom. 4:5). The only persons God saves are the ungodly, wicked persons who believe on the Lord Jesus Christ. Paul writes that the Lord Jesus "was delivered for our offences and was raised again for our justification" (Rom. 4:25).

Jesus Christ is, therefore, our righteousness (I Cor. 1:30). The believer is by God's judicial act acquitted from guilt and restored to divine favor. A reading of the Scriptures discloses that the law demanded perfect righteousness (James 2:10), but man could not himself provide it (Rom. 8:8). What man could not do, however, the grace of God has done (Titus 3:7). This righteousness provided by grace is appropriated by faith (Rom. 5:1), and demonstrated by good works (Jas. 2:21–24). Thus, God's grace is seen as the first cause of justification (Titus 3:7), the blood of Christ as the meritorious cause (Rom. 5:9), faith as the instrumental cause

(Rom. 3:24–26), and good works the proof of justification (Jas. 2:14–26).

The words "justify" and/or "justification" are not in Peter's vocabulary. He speaks of remission but not of justification. To Cornelius Peter said: "To him give all the prophets witness, that through his name whosoever believeth in him shall receive remission of sins" (Acts 10:43). Paul's testimony was stronger, "Be it known unto you therefore, men and brethren, that through this man is preached unto you the forgiveness of sins: and by him all that believe are justified from all things from which ye could not be justified by the law of Moses" (Acts 13:38, 39).

David knew the blessing of justification when he wrote: "Blessed is the man unto whom the Lord imputeth not iniquity" (Ps. 32:2). Connected with justification is the use of the word *impute*, meaning "to reckon." Three instances of the use of imputation are found: Adam's sin is imputed to his posterity because we were all in Adam (Rom. 5:12); our sins were imputed to Christ because He identified Himself with us to become our Saviour (II Cor. 5:21); and the righteousness of God which He provided is imputed to believers (II Cor. 5:21).

One of the finest illustrations of imputed righteousness is found in Balaam's statement to Balak (Num. 23:21). Balak had desired the prophet Balaam to curse Israel, but Balaam said concerning the Lord: "He hath not beheld iniquity in Jacob, neither hath he seen perverseness in Israel." As a nation Israel had appropriated the blood of the Passover lamb (Exod. 12) and God looked at the nation in the light of that sacrifice. The words of Balaam did not mean that Israel was faultless; for the people had murmured against Moses and against the Lord, and the Lord had disciplined them by sending fiery serpents so that many of the people died (Num. 21:5, 6). As far as their standing was concerned, Israel was righteous in God's eyes, but as their Redeemer God, He chastened them because of their disobedience.

There are two elements in justification: the first is remission of punishment, by which God acquits the ungodly who believe in Jesus Christ and declares them just, not innocent. The demands of the law have been satisfied with regard to believers and they are no longer under condemnation (Rom. 8:1). The second is restoration to favor, in which God treats the sinner who believes on the Lord Jesus as if he were personally righteous. God is morally right in justifying the believer because at the same instant he is justified, he is also regenerated, and the process of sanctification is begun by which he is ultimately to be made perfectly holy. Justification is always accompanied by regeneration and union with Christ. There are no degrees in justification. Before the acceptance of Christ as Saviour the sinner is condemned; at the moment of the acceptance of Christ, the believer is reckoned absolutely righteous. The act is instantaneous, complete, and decisive.

In the work of redemption the Lord Jesus Christ paid the ransom price for us in His own death upon Calvary. Having bought us, He is now in the process of accomplishing His eternal purpose with respect to the redeemed. The pattern man, the Lord Jesus, is now at the right hand of the throne of God. Believers have been predestined "to be conformed to the image of His Son" (Rom. 8:29). Some one has said that God was so perfectly pleased with the Lord Jesus that He purposed to make a whole race of beings just like Him. Sanctification is that continuing process of making believers holy which God begins in regeneration and consummates in glorification. It is the work of the Holy Spirit in the lives of believers conforming them unto the image of Jesus Christ.

One may raise the question as to why certain passages of Scripture refer to sanctification as already accomplished. The answer is that at times God calls things which are not as though they were (Rom. 4:17). As far as the purpose of God is concerned, sanctification is already accomplished by our union with Christ. So we read in I Corinthians 1:30, 31: "But of him are ye in Christ Jesus, who of God is made unto us wisdom, and righteousness, and sanctification, and redemption." Just as the position of the believer is that of being justified in Christ, so he is also sanctified in Christ.

From the experiential side, however, sanctification is a progressive experience. Sanctification as a process, however, does not always move ahead at a regular pace. Sometimes great strides are made quickly, and at other times there seems to be no progress because of inner conflict. The Christian has two natures: the old nature which he has because he is a member of the human family, and the new nature which he possesses because he has been born anew by the Spirit. "The flesh lusteth against the Spirit and the Spirit against the flesh . . . that ye may not do the things that ye would" (Gal. 5:17). The old nature is not eradicated while we are in this life, although if we walk in the Spirit we shall not fulfill its desires. God has made provision in Christ for living victoriously over the desires of the flesh and the world and the devil, by being yielded to the control of the Spirit.

Just as the Holy Spirit is the efficient cause in regeneration, so He also is in sanctification. Paul tells us how we are made holy: "But we all with unveiled face beholding as in a mirror the glory of the Lord, are being changed into the same image from one degree of glory unto another by the

Spirit of the Lord" (II Cor. 3:18 ARV). The instrument
that the Holy Spirit uses in our sanctification is the Word of
God. In the Scriptures we see reflected the person of our
Lord Jesus Christ and, as we behold Him, we are changed
into His image. No Christian has ever made great progress in
holiness apart from feeding his soul upon the Word of God.
As in conversion faith is operative, so in sanctification: "As
ye have therefore received Christ Jesus the Lord, so walk
ye in him: rooted and built up in him, and established in
the faith" (Col. 2:6, 7). Faith appropriates all that Christ
offers to us in the Word. Life is to be so completely con-
trolled by Him that every thought is to be brought into
captivity to the obedience of Christ (II Cor. 10:5).

The High Priestly work of our Lord is also related to
sanctification. His intercession in heaven is for the saints,
His death on the cross was in behalf of sinners. In Israel,
the high priest made intercession, not for the Gentiles, but
for Israel in covenant relationship with Jehovah. So now,
our High Priest ministers in heaven to mediate unto us the
benefits of His sacrifice for sins: "Wherefore he is able also
to save them to the uttermost that come unto God by him,
seeing he ever liveth to make intercession for them" (Heb.
7:25). His prayer for believers was: "Sanctify them through
thy truth: thy word is truth" (John 17:17).

The work of sanctification will not be completed in believers until the Lord Jesus comes again: "Now are we the
children of God, and it doth not yet appear what we shall
be: but we know that, when he shall appear, we shall be
like him; for we shall see him as he is" (I John 3:2 ARV).
Our sanctification is to be completed in glorification when
we shall be like him: "We who have the first fruits of the
Spirit groan within ourselves, waiting for the adoption, to
wit, the redemption of our body" (Rom. 8:23).

Our souls are redeemed and our bodies are to be redeemed at the coming of the Lord. Meanwhile as we wait for Him, we are to do as He did. He served; we also are to serve our generation and beseech sinners to be reconciled to God while we wait for His Son from heaven.

FIVE

CHRIST IN THE BELIEVER

BILLY GRAHAM

*Billy Graham is probably the best-known alumnus of
Wheaton College. After receiving his A.B. degree, he
accepted the pastorate of the Baptist Church in Western
Springs, Illinois, which he left in 1946 to become an
evangelist with Youth for Christ. Today he is an evangelist with a world-wide mission, having conducted campaigns in Los Angeles, New York, London, Glasgow,
Paris, Melbourne, and Sydney. He is the author of several
books, including* Peace with God *(1953) and* The Secret
of Happiness *(1955), and of syndicated columns for
newspapers.*

Down on my father's farm there used to be a hired
man who was also a lay preacher. His theology often made
up in color what it lacked in correctness. Frequently on his
way home from work he stopped at the house to "deliver
himself of a sermon." One evening, as we were talking under
a mimosa tree, old Will began to discourse on sanctification.

"Sanctification is a wonderful thing," he said. "The wonderful thing about it is that you can pick it up, and you can
put it down."

Noting that his audience looked puzzled, he hastened to explain his statement. A few nights before, when he came home for supper, his wife called him a name that displeased him. Before he realized what he was doing, he picked up a plate, and hit her on the head with it. For him the quarrel was only an interlude in which he "laid down" his sanctification temporarily.

His hearers enjoyed a hearty laugh at his expense, but entertained afterwards the sober reflection that many Christians live as if they believed as old Will believed, that sanctification is something to be picked up and laid down to suit the situation.

God has called every Christian to a life of sanctification. Yet very few have any idea what it is all about. The subject of sanctification is one of the most neglected truths in the entire Scriptures. The average Christian has become so enmeshed in the things of the world that a call to sanctification leaves him casual or uninterested. Yet at the same time, millions of Christians are aware that something is missing in their lives. They have found that the Christian life is not all that it should be. Many Christians read the New Testament or the story of great saints and find themselves falling far short of what they read on the pages of Scripture or history. The average Christian tries to live the Christian life but finds that the odds are overwhelming. Many fall back into the old ways and their lives are little different from the unbelieving world around them.

The dictionary defines *sanctification* as follows: To make holy; specifically, to make free from sin. Purify; to set apart as holy; to consecrate. To make sacred or inviolable; to make productive of spiritual blessing.

The noun *sanctification* does not occur in the Old Testament, but is found ten times in the Greek New Testament

(Rom. 6:19, 22; I Cor. 1:30; I Thess. 4:3, 4, 7; II Thess. 2:13; I Tim. 2:15; Heb. 12:14; I Peter 1:2). The Greek word employed is *hagiasmos*. The word *hagiosune*, which means "holiness" as is translated in the American Standard Version, occurs three times in the New Testament (Rom. 1:4; II Cor. 7:1; I Thess. 3:13). The verb *hagiazo*, which means "to hallow" or "make holy," occurs twenty-eight times. The adjective *hagios*, which means to be "pure," "consecrated," or "dedicated," appears 235 times in the New Testament. Sanctification may be defined, in both a theological and secular sense, as separation to God, cleansing from moral evil, and conformation to the image of Christ.

It is significant that the word *sanctification* is not used in the Scriptures as an act of grace performed by God in individual lives before Christ's death and resurrection. "Sanctify" in the Old Testament sense was usually something that man did for God; to wit, the designation of animate or inanimate things for sacred use. But "sanctification" in the New Testament sense is something that God does for man.

Sanctification is the glorious companion of justification. Unfortunately, the meaning and means of this precious doctrine have not always been clear in the mind of the church; and because our conception of it has been nebulous, we have neglected to exhort each other to "follow peace with all men, and holiness, without which no man shall see the Lord."

Silence in regard to sanctification, from both pulpit and pew, is doubtless responsible for the failure of many professed Christians to live separated, dedicated, disciplined lives. Every Christian must realize, down in his heart, that a life of triumph and victory is his inalienable birthright. The New Testament is filled with such glowing promises as: "We are more than conquerors through Him that loved us";

"Thanks be unto God, which always causeth us to triumph in Christ"; and "If the Spirit that raised up Jesus from the dead dwell in you, he that raised up Christ from the dead shall also quicken your mortal bodies."

These inspired glimpses of a life "hid with Christ in God" are far different from the weak witnessing, the faltering, and the failures of so many modern Christians. When we compare the casualness and the bungling attempts of twentieth-century disciples with those dynamic, earth-shaking, fearless disciples of the first century, we become painfully aware that we are living beneath our privileges in Christ.

THE WORK OF GOD'S GRACE

The Westminster Catechism (Q. 35) defines sanctification as follows: "Sanctification is the work of God's free grace, whereby we are renewed in the whole man after the image of God, and are enabled more and more to die unto sin, and live unto righteousness." "The work of God's free grace" harmonizes with the classic Biblical references to the doctrine. "Ye are washed . . . ye are sanctified . . . by the Spirit of our God" (I Cor. 6:11). "The very God of peace sanctify you wholly" (I Thess. 5:23). "God hath . . . chosen you to salvation through sanctification of the Spirit" (II Thess. 2:13).

Oftentimes we have become entangled in the very natural but dangerous business of trying to put sanctification on some other basis than grace: sanctification by works, sanctification by will power, sanctification by separation, et cetera. While the will of man is prerequisite as in justification, and though separation is one of the fruits of sanctification, it is "God" who fulfills "all the good pleasure of his goodness

. . . according to the grace of our God and the Lord Jesus Christ" (II Thess. 1:11, 12).

It is obvious to any student of the gospel that sanctification is a God-imparted work of grace (II Cor. 5:18); that it was bought by Christ and wrought by the Spirit (I Peter 1:2); that it was not just for Christ's immediate disciples (Eph. 5:26); that it is the will of God for every believer to be sanctified (I Thess. 4:3); that it makes us vessels of honor (II Tim. 2:21); and that Christ's earnest prayer was that His disciples be "sanctified" (John 17:7).

A WALK IN THE LIGHT

The sanctified life is a walk in the light. "For ye were sometimes darkness, but now are ye light in the Lord: walk as children of light" (Eph. 5:8). "If we walk in the light, as he is in the light, we have fellowship one with another, and the blood of Jesus Christ . . . cleanseth us from all sin" (I John 1:7). Confession and cleansing take place in the light. When do we come into the light? When we walk in the fellowship of Him who is the Light of the world! When we are justified by faith, we emerge from the dark shadows of self-deception into the glorious light of Christ. This is the launching power that sends the believer into an eternal orbit and an exciting adventure of growth and fellowship with Christ. In this realm, black is black and white is white. God is light; and when a man brings his life out into the light, he is seen for what he really is (John 3:19, 20). "In the dark," as the French proverb goes, "all cats are gray." When a man is in darkness, standards are indistinguishable and it is easy to look around and say to himself, "I'm not so bad; I'm as good as the next fellow."

As children of the light, we realize that we are not

measured by the next fellow but by Christ. The nearer we draw to Him, the more aware are we of our imperfections. When we confess that we do not know, then we are ready to be taught by the Spirit of Christ (I Cor. 8:2).

When we become aware of our spiritual poverty, and hunger and thirst after righteousness, then the Holy Spirit can fill us with Himself (Matt. 5:6). When we covet His Presence more than any earthly possession, He favors us by filling the vacuum of our hearts with His fullness. As Melville B. Cox, the great early American Methodist, wrote in his journal: "I do not think that I am sanctified, but I am groaning for it. I want a holy heart. And He who has begotten the struggle for it, I trust, will grant it unto me. I want to know all that a man can know of God and live." [1]

The greatest obstacle to our sanctification is our unwillingness to see things as they are, and particularly to see ourselves as we really are. As the old Scottish couplet of Robert Burns goes:

> Would some power the giftie gi'e us,
> To see ourselves as others see us.

If we could just see ourselves as God sees us, then our souls would groan to be made into the image of Christ! Until we come out into the light and acknowledge our need for holiness, God will not unleash in us the supernatural, sanctifying power of His Holy Spirit. Many of the movie queens appear as glamorous as they do only because they and the directors and the photographers are careful to present them only in a flattering light, from complimentary angles. Quite a number of flaws can be concealed in this way. But we cannot play this game with God! Many Christians try to straddle the line between darkness and light so that they can consider themselves in some relation to God and so the shadows fall in a flattering way upon them. But when "we say that we have no sin, we deceive ourselves, and the truth is not in us" (I John 1:8). When we make an effort to use subterfuge with God, the result is self-deception.

When we "walk in the light," we have fellowship with God, because no effort is made to camouflage or deceive. He knows the worst about us — even the innermost shame that we hide from our best friends. But He meets that worst with His best and continues to work in us, "both to will and to do of his good pleasure" (Phil. 2:13). Now we are children of the light! Having been brought out into the light, we are ready to grow, develop, and mature.

> 'Tis done, the great transaction's done,
> I am the Lord's, and He is mine.
> He drew me and I followed on,
> Charmed to confess the voice divine.

There are two principals, or persons, involved in sanctification: God and man. Just as in justification, man is the recipient and God the giver. Grace is free, but there are always the means of grace to be employed. A man was given a castle in Scotland, but he had to spend quite a lot of money to acquire the gift. He had to buy a ticket, have papers drawn up, prove his identity, et cetera. God gives us justification and sanctification, but this does not imply that we are passive ingrates, utterly lacking in the powers of gratitude and reciprocation. Christ has never given salvation to an unwilling receiver. Just so, He does not impart the grace of sanctification to passive, inert professors of religion. We must hunger and thirst after righteousness before we can be filled.

Let us begin by thinking of God's part in our sanctification. The Father, Son, and Holy Spirit all play their part in our sanctification. So great and important is the sanctification of the believer that the Trinity unites to bring it to pass in our lives. God's part is the imputation of Christ as: (1) our righteousness and (2) our sanctification. "But of him are ye in Christ Jesus, who of God is made unto us . . . righteousness, and sanctification . . ." (I Cor. 1:30). When we are justified by faith, or "in Christ," God attributes Christ's righteousness to us. And in our sanctification He imputes His holiness to us.

In Jesus' most impassioned prayer for His disciples He prayed, "Sanctify them through thy truth" (John 17:17). If holiness represents the state of heart and life in conformity with God's will, then sanctification is the act or process by which this state is wrought. And it is God who sanctifies. "It is God which worketh in you both to will and to work" (Phil. 2:13).

Regeneration is the implanting of new life in man by God. Sanctification is the perpetuity of this new life, a blessed continuance of God's grace within us wherein we are conformed into the image of Christ.

The Second Person of the Trinity, Christ, sanctifies the believer by laying down His life for him. "By the which will we are sanctified through the offering of the body of Jesus Christ" (Heb. 10:10). "Wherefore Jesus also, that he might sanctify the people with his own blood, suffered without the gate" (Heb. 13:12). Our sanctification began at the cross where Christ purchased our right and privilege to be sanctified. The pouring out of Christ's precious blood on Calvary was for a twofold purpose: first, to redeem us from sin, and second, to sanctify us unto holiness. "Christ also loved the church, and gave himself for it; that he might sanctify and cleanse it with the washing of water by the word . . . that it should be holy and without blemish" (Eph. 5:25, 26, 27).

The Holy Spirit, the Third Person of the Trinity, sanctifies the believer that he may triumph over the carnal nature. "For the law of the Spirit of life in Christ Jesus hath made me free from the law of sin and death" (Rom. 8:2). The Holy Spirit in the life of the believer provides the balance of power in the struggle of life over death.

Regeneration presupposes the presence of the Holy Spirit in the life of the believer. So far as that is a new life from God it is *ipso facto* holy.[2] There can be no spiritual life apart from the presence of the Spirit. Hence we can say that every believer possesses the Holy Spirit. And since the Holy Spirit is not a quantity but a Person, it follows that every believer may have complete fellowship with Him. But we cannot always assume that the Spirit possesses all of the believer. Sanctification is the act (first) and the process (second) whereby we become possessed of Him. Unless the believer moves progressively in this glorious process, he is not developing normally toward the goal of ultimate holiness, perfect love, and conformity to the image of Christ.

Having observed the function of the three persons in the Godhead regarding our sanctification, let us proceed to sanctification as man's task. All Christian life is summed up in this Biblical ethic: "Work out your own salvation with fear and trembling. For it is God which worketh in you both to will and to do of his good pleasure" (Phil. 2:12, 13). As Dr. Arthur Way puts it in his *Letters of St. Paul:* "You have not to do it in your unaided strength; it is God who is all the while supplying the impulse, giving you the power to resolve, the strength to perform, the execution of His good pleasure."

Practically every promise in Scripture is coupled with a condition. For example, "If we confess . . . he [will] forgive" (I John 1:9); "If we walk in the light . . . the blood of

Jesus Christ cleanseth" (I John 1:7); "Having therefore these promises . . . let us cleanse ourselves from all filthiness of the flesh" (II Cor. 7:1); and "follow peace with all men, and holiness, without which no man shall see the Lord" (Heb. 12:14). Confession on man's part is matched by forgiveness on God's part. As in the story of the prodigal, when we as erring, hungry sons take a step toward a forgiving Father, we find He is already on the way to welcome us. This is true of every grace. God gives out, and we live it out. It is God who "worketh" within us, but it is our obligation to be a worthy outlet of God's goodness and grace. In this way we "work out" our "salvation." As we manifest Christ, God replenishes the supply. Hence, as the *Westminster Catechism* says, justification is "the gift," but sanctification is "the work." God not only gives but He keeps on giving. His responsibility is giving and ours is living. As we are faithful on our part, so we grow, and more and more develop into the image of Christ.

We must always keep in mind that the heart of the believer is a battleground and will remain so until death. In us the Holy Spirit of God is fighting against the flesh. Just as the enzymes in the blood stream of a grub attack and destroy the old organs that were used in its life of crawling, and build up the organs needed for its new life of flying as a butterfly, so the Holy Spirit works within us to transform us into Christ's image. By and through the miracle of sanctification, we are changed from the grub-like sons of Adam to sons of God: from slaves of sin to sons of righteousness and holiness.

In this transforming process, which begins at regeneration and continues progressively in sanctification, there are certain responsibilities imposed upon man, as we have already indicated. We might call these hints toward holiness or signs directed to sanctification.

The first is: "Put ye on the Lord Jesus Christ, and make not provision for the flesh, to fulfill the lusts thereof" (Romans 13:14).

When someone asked Donald O'Connor's advice on how to stop smoking, he answered, "Carry wet matches." We are to co-operate with God in removing the means of igniting the fleshly flame that flares up within us. Robert Murray McCheyne of Dundee (d. 1843) says, "Avoid the occasion for sin as much as the sin itself." Whatever the sins may be that you feel the Holy Spirit is trying to take from your life, be sure you are not taking the side of the flesh by making provision for its lusts. Do not dwell on the thoughts that lead to sinful action. Do not read books that give rise to sinful thoughts. Do not acquire any literature that stimulates fleshly thoughts; and if you have any of it in your library, get rid of it.

A young Christian in England approached a wise old Christian about a besetting sin of his.

"I think," he exclaimed in desperation, "I think I shall die if I cannot have some. What shall I do?"

"Die then," the old saint replied.

When we reach the place where we would rather die than do that which would dishonor our Lord, victory is ours.

Whatever your besetting sin may be, there is something you can do in your moments of strength that will make it harder for you to fall in your moments of weakness. If there are material accessories that are stunting your growth in Christ, get rid of them. A financial loss is much less serious than a spiritual tragedy. The Bible says, if your eye causes you to offend, pluck it out. If you have become attached to the wrong social group, pull up stakes and move to another town if need be. Lot should have moved out of Sodom long before the angel uprooted him. He had no business to go there in the first place. For unworthy reasons, such as love of money or the search of social prestige, many Christians have moved to where they are now living. Whatever the cost, make sure that you are not contributing to circumstances that make it easier for you to sin and harder for you to live a holy life. "Make not provision for the flesh, to fulfil the lusts thereof" (Romans 13:14 ARV).

The second valuable directive toward sanctification and a holy life is: The putting off of the old man and the putting on of the new.

"That ye put off . . . the old man, which is corrupt according to the deceitful lusts . . . and that ye put on the new man, which after God is created in righteousness and true holiness" (Eph. 4:22–24). The power to "put off" is given of God, but the act of "putting off" is our responsibility. The more we put off the old nature, the more we are enabled to put on the new. In this connection there is a remarkable series of contrasts in the Ephesian Epistle.

Put off deceit and put on the truth. "Wherefore putting away lying, speak every man truth with his neighbor" (Eph. 4:25). It is understandable why the Apostle should put this first, because honesty and integrity are most essential in the sanctified life.

Put off resentment and put on reconciliation. "Be ye angry, and sin not: let not the sun go down upon your wrath" (Eph. 4:26). This indicates that there is a place for sanctified indignation, but it is justified only when wrong has been done to another. The weak way would be to do nothing about it or to wait a day or two. But the "new man" is to attend to it right away so that no place can be given to the Devil.

Put off stealing and put on honest labor. "Let him that stole steal no more: but rather let him labor, working with his hands the thing which is good, that he may have to give to him that needeth" (Eph. 4:28). Here the Apostle indicates that there are three ways of acquiring anything. You may steal, or you may labor, or you may receive it as a gift. The impulse of the new man is to give, but that means that he must engage in honest toil so he will have the wherewithal. There are three philosophies of life. The first is: What's yours is mine and I am going to take it. That's the gangster philosophy. The second is: What's mine is mine and I am going to keep it. That's the miser's philosophy. The third is: What's mine is Christ's and I'll share it. That is the Christian philosophy. The sanctified life is an outflowing life: a life of sharing the material and spiritual gifts of God.

Put off carnal talk and put on edifying speech. "Let no corrupt communication proceed out of your mouth, but that which is good to the use of edifying" (Eph. 4:29). The word *corrupt* as used here means "damaging or mischievous speech, designed to hurt or tear down another." The heart of Christ must bleed at the backbiting, the slander, and the idle gossip in which so many professed Christians engage. We are to put off corrupt communication and put on edifying speech. This is a mark of those who are sanctified.

A further sobering thought lies in the fact that the Bible says that some day we will give account of every word. Who would have thought a few years ago that man would be able to pull voices out of the air as radio and television are doing? It is a known fact that no sound uttered is ever lost. The vibrations continue somewhere, like tiny wavelets caused by a little pebble dropped in some eternal sea. Even now we are told scientists are working on a device that will pull voices out of the past. How would you like to have everything you have ever said about others pulled out of the air and played aloud for those persons to hear? Just how it will happen we do not know, but we can be sure of one thing: we will have to give an account some day of every idle word.

Put off bitterness and put on kindness. "Let all bitterness . . . be put away from you. . . . And be ye kind one to another . . . even as God for Christ's sake hath forgiven you" (Eph. 4:31, 32). One of the ways you can test your sanctification is by examining your relations to fellow Christians. The Bible says, "He who does not love his brother whom he has seen, how can he love God whom he has not seen?" Most of us are so full of self-love that we can have fellowship only with those who are exactly like us: our identical twins, so to speak. But in the great family of God there is a wide variation of personality, and we must love them all, their faults notwithstanding.

Put off impurity and put on purity. "But fornication, and all uncleanness, or covetousness, let it not be once named among you, as becometh saints . . . For the fruit of the Spirit is in all goodness and righteousness and truth" (Eph. 5:3, 9). Only as we become emptied of impure thoughts, impure conversation, and impure attitudes can the Holy Spirit perform His purifying work of "goodness, righteousness and truth" in our hearts. The verbs *shun, avoid,* and *abstain,* which are employed in the apostolic admonitions, indicate that the believer has a responsibility in his sanctification. God puts the beauty in the rose, but we must cull out the weeds that the flower of holiness may come into full bloom.

Put off foolishness and put on wisdom. "See then that ye

walk circumspectly, not as fools, but as wise" (Eph. 5:15). A good motto for the Christian should be: No conformity to the world; no compromise with the Devil; and no confidence in the flesh. The greatest wisdom is to know what the will of the Lord is for your life. You may master your trade, you may go to the top in your profession, you may be called a great success in life; but if you are living out of the will of God, then, in God's eyes, you have failed. With that in mind, Paul says, "Be ye not unwise, but understanding what the will of the Lord is" (Eph. 5:17). And what is the will of God for the Christian? The answer echoes back from the courts of heaven, "This is the will of God, even your sanctification" (I Thess. 4:3). God wants His children to be His "separated ones," which they surely are because Christ purchased them with His own blood. But He also wants them to be His volitionally: fully yielded vessels of honor and meet for the Master's use.

The third step toward sanctification is: self-denial. Jesus said, "If any man will come after me, let him deny himself" (Luke 9:23).

The Greek word used for denial is used only a few times in the New Testament. Probably you have already thought of one instance — the story of Peter's denial of his Lord. Christ was on trial. What did Peter do? Christ was being mocked, and beaten, and falsely accused. Did Peter mock Him? Did Peter beat Him? Did Peter falsely accuse Him? No. All Peter did was to stand by and do nothing. He said that he did not even know Him and refused to have anything to do with Him. Peter could have rushed into the court room and testified that the accusations were false. He could have said that for years Jesus had gone about doing good, healing the sick, and raising the dead. But he did none of these things. He did not want to get involved. This is how Peter denied Christ.

But what happens when we are mocked? How do we react when we are beaten? What do we do when we are falsely accused? We leap to our defense, always eager to put ourselves in the best light. We recite our entire list of good deeds, though they be irrelevant to the question at hand. We try to distract attention and change the subject. We fight back with everything we have. This is what God hates and what hinders our sanctification. God calls on us not to defend ourselves but to deny ourselves. When we are slighted or ridiculed or even falsely accused, we should refuse to get involved. Our reputation will probably suffer for a while. We will leave slanders unanswered. We may lose a friend or two. Our pride will suffer. Our glory will be diminished. But all of this is a necessary part of the death of self that must come before we can be fashioned after Christ's own image. Our egos must be crucified daily. Self must be nailed to the cross.

The word *deny* is again used in Peter's sermon on the porch of the temple as recorded in Acts 3. Peter tells the crowd that they denied the Holy One in the presence of Pilate. What had the crowd done? They had shouted passionately, "We will not have this man to reign over us!" (Luke 19:14). Self-denial means that you must take this stand concerning yourself. You must cry with equal vigor, "I will not have me to reign over myself!" There must be a day-by-day recognition that we are not our own masters; Jesus Christ is Lord, even of our own selves.

In Acts 7 we find the word again, as Stephen reminds his hearers that their fathers denied Moses in Egypt saying, "Who made you to be a ruler and a judge over us?" As the ordinary duties and circumstances of life engage our atten-

tion, little by little we often find ourselves slipping into a
pattern of ignoring the Lordship of Christ and acting without reference to Him who is the judge of all things. In
moments like these we must catch ourselves short and deny
ourselves by saying, "Wait a minute! Who made me to be
a ruler and a judge over me?" Christ is our Ruler and Judge,
and self-justification, or self-condemnation for that matter,
has no place among those who are sanctified. Only the Judge
can justify; and only the Judge can condemn. When we recognize this fact and put our case completely in His hands,
we are approaching the state of perfect trust.

Self-denial does not imply that the Christian is hedged in
by moral scruples of a negative kind, cramped within narrow
limits too small for the soul of man. The healthy Christian
life is the opposite of the restricted life. It is a life abandoned
to God, full of happy holiness and holy happiness.

To recapitulate, the sanctified soul completely denies self
and opens all the windows of his heart toward God. His
whole being is oriented toward God, His ways, His will, and
His work. The total personality is brought under the control
of the Spirit.

A *fourth sign-post on the road to sanctification is found
in Romans* 12:2: *"And be not conformed to this world; but
be ye transformed by the renewing of your mind."* Phillips
interprets it in this way, "Don't let the world around you
squeeze you into its mold." The cold, deadening power of
the mold is dreadfully active in America today.

In his book, *The Organization Man*, William Whyte, Jr.,
describes modern man not as a man who has made the
world but as a man who has conformed to the world he lives
in. Being conformed to the world dwarfs personality, breeds
boredom, and makes men after their own image rather than

God's. It has been well said, "Everyone is born an original and dies a copy." We must not yield one hair's breadth to the fatal pressures of the world. For the world (this age), with its materialism and its superficiality, is the sworn, relentless enemy of all real Christian holiness. The Christian goes into the world with the same precaution that a surgeon enters the operating room. He goes in with a sense of mission. He goes in properly safeguarded against contamination. He goes in to help the sick and dying.

As Dr. Griffith Thomas has said, "The world is not so much a sphere as an atmosphere." In its atmosphere are germs that attack our spiritual health. We are not to hide away in a cloistered place of seclusion, but we are to go out into the world as worthy representatives of the most high God, in the spirit of love and true holiness; all the while seeking that transformation that comes by the renewing of our minds: "That is," as the Amplified New Testament puts it, "by its new ideas and its new attitude — so that you may prove (for yourselves) what is the good and acceptable and perfect will of God." This is what God desires for each of us. Not so much our service but our growing in likeness to His Son. Not to work for Him so much as to walk with Him.

CHRISTIAN PERFECTION

In discussing the subject of sanctification, the question always arises: Is it perfect and entire? There is much misunderstanding here. Indeed, the Calvinists and the Arminians seem to clash head-on at this point. But when one makes a close study of the two viewpoints, there is much that harmonizes them. There is a difference between perfect love and sinless perfection. True holiness and sanctification are ultimate goals in both interpretations. "To the end he may stablish your hearts unblameable in holiness before God, even our Father, at the coming of our Lord Jesus Christ with all his saints" (I Thess. 3:13).

If the holy life is God's requirement and at the same time His deed, why then should sanctification not be the goal and privilege of every child of God? Wesley's teaching of "perfect love" is not perfection of degree but of kind. In the Wesleyan concept of the doctrine, sanctification is gradual, and entire sanctification is instantaneous. In the converse view, believers are sanctified instantaneously when they are regenerated, but complete sanctification is progressive. The end result is the same. The only difference is the means to the end.

The test of any doctrine is what it produces in human experience. On March 6, 1760, John Wesley, founder of the Methodist Church, enters in his *Journal* the following testimony of one Elizabeth Longmore: "I felt my soul was all love. I was so stayed on God as I never felt before, and knew that I loved Him with all my heart . . . and the witness that God had saved me from my sins grew clearer every hour. I have never since found my heart wander from God." Wesley makes this comment, "Now this is what I always did, and do now, mean by Christian perfection. And this I believe many have attained, on the same evidence that I believe many are justified." [3]

Charles G. Finney also believed and taught that the Christian should live a life of holiness and separation. In his sermon "Victory over the World through Faith," he says, "He who does not habitually overcome the world is not born of God. In saying this, I do not intend to affirm that a true Christian may not sometimes be overcome by sin; but I do affirm that overcoming the world is the general rule, and falling into sin is only the exception. Many engage in the very opposite expectation. . . . How perfectly chilling and horrible for persons to oppose the idea of expecting deliverance from sin and yet talk calmly of going on in sin all the rest of their earthly days." [4]

God's part in our sanctification is perfect and entire, for "He doeth all things well." But as for our part we must always remember that, "We have this treasure in earthen vessels, that the excellency of the power may be of God, and not of us" (II Cor. 4:7). We boast not in what we are, for we are yet in the flesh, but we glory in what we are becoming through His sanctifying grace.

This close walk with God which produces holiness of heart and life in the believer is a far cry from the modern conception of what a life "hid with Christ in God" is. In neglecting the teaching, the preaching, and the living of this precious doctrine, we have failed to represent properly to the world the joy of being in Christ and led by the Spirit.

Theodore Monod's hymn beautifully expresses the progressive walk of sanctification and holiness:

> Oh, the bitter pain and sorrow
> That a time could ever be,
> When I proudly said to Jesus,
> "All of self, and none of Thee."
>
> Yet He found me; I beheld Him
> Bleeding on th' accursed tree,
> And my wistful heart said faintly,
> "Some of self, and some of Thee."
>
> Day by day His tender mercy
> Healing, helping, full and free,
> Bro't me lower, while I whispered,
> "Less of self, and more of Thee."

Higher than the highest heavens,
Deeper than the deepest sea,
Lord, Thy love at last has conquered,
"None of self, and all of Thee."

Thus we have seen that God's supreme desire and purpose is that we might be sanctified. This supreme desire of God led to the creation of the universe. This supreme desire which God has cherished in His heart from all eternity is a paternalistic desire which reveals itself throughout all of Scripture. It is God's desire that He might share with us, through us, and in us, His highest ambitions and longings. He has chosen to share His image, His life, His nature, His love, His holiness, His fellowship, and ultimately His throne with those of us who are in Christ Jesus. This is His ultimate purpose in creation and in redemption. The Apostle Paul writing in Ephesians chose to call it "the mystery of His will."

In reading Betty Elliot's best-seller, *Shadow of the Almighty*, I am again impressed that whether our lives are long or short, our daily purpose and objective should be that Christ's image may be formed in us. In 1948, while a student at Wheaton, Jim Elliot wrote, "Father, take my life, yea, my blood if Thou wilt, and consume it with Thine enveloping fire. I would not save it, for it is not mine to save. Have it, Lord, have it all. Pour out my life as an oblation for the world. Blood is only of value as it flows before Thine altar."

When Jim Elliot was martyred, the material things he left behind were few: a small home in the jungle, a few well-worn clothes, books, and tools. To the world it was not much of a legacy, but Jim from his earliest days had allowed Christ to be formed in him and had put into daily practice His commandments.

SIX

THE CHURCH OF GOD

GLENN W. BARKER

Glenn W. Barker was graduated from Wheaton College (A.B.) and from Wheaton Graduate School (A.M.). He is now Professor of New Testament at Gordon Divinity School, Beverly Farms, Massachusetts.

Not since the Reformation has there been so great an interest in the unity of the church as there is today. From the hour when Martin Luther nailed his theses to the church door in Wittenberg down to the present century, Christian believers have been engaged in independent reforming movements. Definitions of doctrines and of polity based on differing interpretations of Scripture and influenced by widely varying historical conditions have tended to separate rather than to unify believers.

Undoubtedly a vigorous diversity of convictions is better that a lax accord of apathy. One may concede that much energy has been wasted and that much unnecessary strife has been created by the petty wars between jarring sects. On the other hand, the divisions of Christendom have reemphasized Scriptural truth, and have enriched the interpretation of the revelation of God by their new, if sometimes tangential, contributions.

The external pressure of paganism and of Communism is now forcing these dissident elements to reconsider their common faith. Can they afford to maintain a mutual alienation as they confront a common enemy, or must they unite for effectiveness? Is it possible to combine their forces without the costly compromise of surrendering essential truth?

These questions have demanded a new consideration of the nature of the church. The problems of the ages have been anticipated in the Word of God. What does it have to say concerning the character and destiny of the church which is the body of Christ? Definition of its nature and purpose is necessary if we are to think straight concerning it.

The Greek word which is translated "church" in the New Testament is *ecclesia*. In secular Greek literature *ecclesia* simply means "assembly" or "gathering of the people" and refers to the regularly summoned assembly of the citizens of a Greek city. The secular usage of the word is exemplified in Acts 19:39, as the town clerk of Ephesus remonstrates with the people that they should refer any actions against Paul's companions to a lawfully constituted *ecclesia* (assembly). Apart from this example, *ecclesia* is used in the New Testament as a theological word designating the company of Christian believers. Cremer offers one of the most useful suggestions for this usage when he defines *ecclesia* as the "redeemed community." [1]

The expression "redeemed community" is particularly helpful because it serves to indicate the character of the inner relationship that exists between the people of God of the Old Testament and the new people of God in Christ. In this regard, *ecclesia* must not be viewed as introducing a concept into the New Testament which is completely foreign to Judaism. Actually, this word is borrowed from the Old Testament Scriptures through the Septuagint. More than a hundred times it appears in this Greek translation of the Old Testament as a rendering for the congregation of Israel. The two Hebrew terms which as a rule are used of the covenant community are '*edhah*' [2] and *qahal*. The latter term came to be preferred more generally by the later Old Testament writers. It is significant that in the seventy-five occurrences of this word, the Septuagint translators used *ecclesia* as its equivalent sixty-nine times. However, it does appear that it is the root idea of calling that binds the concepts together.

The Old Testament *qahal* was established when God summoned the nation of Israel at Mt. Sinai, and by His voice, that is, by His own word, the covenant community was created. This time was later referred to in Judaism as "the day of *qahal*." *Qahal* came in time to denote the Old Testament congregation "actively engaged in God's purpose of revelation and salvation, that is, caught up in the mighty events whereby God intervenes redemptively in history and involved in the forward thrust of the covenant toward final and universal fulfillment." [3] Correspondingly, the New Testament *qahal* or *ecclesia* was duly summoned of God by His own Divine Word, the Eternal Logos. It, too, had been ordered into existence as a "covenant" community, and, likewise receiving the new covenant in Jesus' blood, was "caught up" in God's great redemptive program. Thus, the believers witnessed by the very choice of their name that they now realized they stood in direct succession to Israel, not in any nationalistic sense, but as inheritors of the hope of Israel.

Support for this conclusion is found in the use of other

familiar expressions which historically refer to Israel. The early Christians are spoken of as the "elect," "Abraham's seed," the "twelve tribes," and "strangers of the dispersion." The birth of the church was recognized by the Christians as a fulfillment in part of the covenant made with Abraham and Moses. With the Israelites God had covenanted that He would establish a people for His own possession who should receive His promises. They would be His "own possession," " a kingdom of priests," "a holy nation," the bearer of His light to the nations (Exod. 19:5, 6). In I Peter it is precisely in these terms that the church of the New Testament is addressed. They are "elect . . . according to the foreknowledge of God the Father, in sanctification of the Spirit, unto obedience and sprinkling of the blood of Jesus Christ" (1:2). They are ". . . elect, precious . . . living stones . . . built up a spiritual house . . . a holy priesthood, to offer up spiritual sacrifices . . ." (2:4, 5). They have become ". . . an elect race, a royal priesthood, a holy nation, a people for God's own possession" (2:9).[4]

It is clear from the whole context that these prophetic words are not to be explained as directed to Christian Jews. Rather, they are addressed specifically to the new community of the redeemed, the church. That this church is predominantly Gentile in character is evident from the next verse: "who in time past were no people, but now are the people of God: who had not obtained mercy, but now have obtained mercy" (2:10).

This does not mean that Peter believed that the existence of the church as such exhausted the promises made to Israel. Nor did he believe that the church was to be understood as the realization of the eternal kingdom of God. Instead, he was declaring the fact that it had taken the place of Israel as the witnessing community. As the people of Israel had been "sojourners" upon the earth awaiting the manifestation of God's eternal kingdom, so Peter now addresses the church as the new "sojourners and pilgrims" (2:11; 1:1), waiting for the appearance of the "Chief Shepherd" (5:4), for the "day of visitation" (2:12) when "his glory shall be revealed" (4:13), when they will receive the inheritance "reserved in heaven" for them (1:4). It would appear then, in this first instance, that the choice of the name, *ecclesia*, was no accident. Rather, it was used to express the genuine conviction of the Christians that they had become the New Community of God.

Secondly, "redeemed community" is particularly helpful as a definition because it reminds us that at the heart of the Biblical concept lies the fact that the church is an actual and "visible" gathering. This conclusion would need no mention except for the fact that today the concept of "invisible church" has become so familiar to us. Unfortunately, the use of the term "invisible" has tended to becloud the central character of the church's existence. Undoubtedly part of the problem lies in the fact that our modern "churches" have become so institutionalized that it scarcely seems possible to apply to them the term "temple of God" or "body of Christ," or "fellowship of the Holy Spirit" without appearing blasphemous.

To a large extent it was this same kind of reaction by the reformers against the Roman Church which led them to use the adjective "invisible" as a more desirable designation of the church. As a term appropriate to express the spiritual nature of the church (Luther), or the universal character of the body of Christ composed of those true believers known only to God (Calvin), the expression "invisible church" may have had some justification. To the extent that the use of this word results in the minimizing of the importance of the visible body of Christ, its usage is ill-advised. Too many have been willing to transfer the duties, privileges, and what is more serious, life in the Holy Spirit, to some "ideal" church whose only existence is in heaven. The detrimental effects of such thinking may readily be observed today in the loss of spiritual life, spiritual power, and spiritual gifts in the church.

Against such a development the Old Testament and the New Testament protest. Even a casual investigation of the Old Testament is sufficient to indicate that God's purpose for Israel was that she become a visible community. Apart from existing in time and space as a manifest witness to the power and glory of God, she would have had no significance. In the same way and to the same extent the purpose of God is unveiled for his church in the New Testament. The calling of "the Twelve" and the sending forth of the Holy Spirit at Pentecost were directed toward the end of establishing a visible historical group. Only such a community could realize the blessings of God, manifest His life, and receive His gifts. This in no way is intended to deny the fact that the church, just because it is a redeemed community, must in one sense include all of those who have by faith a share in the redemption of God. This great invisible host, glorious as it may be, is not called to effect the purposes of God. It is to God's visible community that this task has been entrusted. As K. L. Schmidt has so pointedly remarked, this community must be "precisely as visible and temporal as the Christian man." [5]

Finally, the term "redeemed community" is an appropriate definition for *ecclesia* because it reminds us that whenever *ecclesia* is used in its technical sense, there is always in accompaniment, either expressed or implied, the qualifying phrase "of God" or "of Christ." The significance of this fact can hardly be overstated. *Ecclesia* is not "church" in any sociological or political sense of assembly. It is never called into being by human ingenuity or as the result of some spontaneous creative act of its own. It is the result of the deliberate choice of God. He alone calls it into existence, and He shapes it according to His own purpose. For this reason it can be spoken of either in the singular or plural. It can be God's "gatherings" in Asia or God's "gathering" at Corinth. The term is just as proper for the smallest group as it is for the whole family of believers. Because the church derives its true significance from the One who gathers rather than from the gathered, there is the guarantee that the church is represented in its completeness in every company of believers. "Where two or three are gathered in my name, there am I in their midst" (Matt. 18:20), and where He is present nothing can be wanting.

THE CHURCH AND THE OLD TESTAMENT

As was suggested in the definition, the redeemed community of the New Testament is dynamically related to that community of the Old. The precise character of this relationship may be expressed simply under the terms "promise" and "fulfillment." God's visible community began with Abraham. To him God said "I will make of thee a great nation, and I will bless thee, and make thy name great; and be thou a blessing" (Gen. 12:2). "And I will establish my covenant between me and thee and thy seed after thee throughout their generations for an everlasting covenant, to be a God unto thee, and to thy seed after thee" (Gen. 17:7). To Moses this covenant was amplified at the time of the giving of the Law: "Now therefore, if ye will obey my voice indeed, and keep my covenant, then ye shall be mine own possession from among all peoples . . . and ye shall be unto me a kingdom of priests, and a holy nation" (Exod. 19:5, 6). So from Abraham came forth a family; out of this family, a tribe; and out of this tribe, a nation.

In spite of the mighty acts and great deliverances which God granted to His people, Israel tended to be unfaithful. Her heart yearned for Egypt; her desire was away from God. The temporal blessings which she enjoyed were powerless to effect a genuine obedience unto God. Although chastened in bondage, scourged by plague, and oppressed by foreign domination, she remained resistant toward the covenant. Yet God did not abandon either His promise or His people. Establishing a faithful remnant, He continued to witness to them of His grace. To this elect group He reiterated by His prophets that though Israel should sin, apostatize, and fail, He would not desert His covenant. If there should be but one faithful Israelite, God would in His time bestow His Kingdom.

Though at best Israel was content to follow only afar off, her understanding, mediated to her by her experiences in history and intensified by her encounter with the word of the prophets, continued to increase. In time she came to realize that God's intention for His people had implications which transcended her greatest expectations. Foremost among these was the fact that Israel's true destiny necessarily lay in the future. The past manifestations to the patriarchs, the deliverance of the nation from Egypt, the temporal blessings which had rained down upon the people, gave mute testimony to the fact that God was preparing a supreme deliverance for his people, of which all past experiences were only fore-shadowings. The promised land, the kingdom of David, the temple at Jerusalem, were only "earnests" or indications of the surpassing glory which should be. Thus Israel became in time an eschatological community whose concern lay with the "end days," the "days of fulfillment," the "age to come."

A second realization, parallel to the first, was that these last days and the fulfillment of the covenant made with Abraham, Isaac, and Jacob could be realized only through a "radical event." Not only would the whole world experience radical change, but Israel, God's own community, would need to be reconstituted in order to receive the promise. This Jeremiah made plain:

Behold, the days come, saith Jehovah, that I will make a new covenant with the house of Israel, and with the house of Judah: not according to the covenant that I made with their fathers . . . But this is the covenant that I will make with the house of Israel after those days, saith Jehovah: I will put my law in their inward parts, and in their heart will I write it; and I will be their God, and they shall be my people. And they shall teach no more every man his neighbor, and every man his brother, saying, Know Jehovah; for they shall all know me, from the least of them unto the greatest of them, saith Jehovah: for I will forgive their iniquity, and their sin will I remember no more (Jer. 31:31–34).

In the fullness of time, God proved His faithfulness and vindicated His Word to Israel. Sending His own Son, He provided the one worthy Israelite who could receive the promise and inherit the eternal kingdom for His people. But He came not according to the speculation of faithless Israel, as a conquering Messiah to establish a temporal kingdom. He came rather as the suffering servant of Isaiah, a "root growing out of dry ground" (Cf. Isa. 53:2). Fulfilling the law, He became a curse for Israel's sake, in order that she might be counted worthy of the promises.

To the people of God, Jesus announced the imminence

of the Kingdom. To questioning Jews he said, "If I by the Spirit of God cast out demons, then is the kingdom of God come upon you" (Matt. 12:28). When John the Baptist inquired whether He was the one to come, Jesus answered him with words Isaiah had used to describe the coming Kingdom of God: "The blind receive their sight, the lame walk, the lepers are cleansed, and the deaf hear, the dead are raised up, the poor have the gospel preached to them. And blessed is he, whosoever shall find no occasion of stumbling in me" (Lk. 7:22, 23, mg., ARV). When the seventy returned from their successful mission to the cities of Israel in which they announced the imminence of the Kingdom of God, Jesus answered their enthusiasm with a Messianic proclamation, "I beheld Satan fallen as lightning from heaven" (Lk. 10:18). Jesus gave other indications that the new covenant to which Jeremiah had borne witness was soon to be in effect. To His disciples He declared that they would shortly receive the Spirit of truth, who would dwell with them and be in them (John 14:17). To the Samaritan woman He stated that "the hour cometh, when neither in this mountain, nor in Jerusalem, shall ye worship the Father . . . But the hour cometh, and now is, when the true worshippers shall worship the Father in spirit and truth . . ." (John 4:21–23). In parables he taught that the old covenant was passing away and the old community was superseded.

When Jesus implied the coming existence of a new community the Jews began to have serious forebodings. That membership in this community was not to be a matter of national descent, that a repentant heart and a new spirit alone would qualify a man before God, could only disturb His hearers. Yet Jesus' disclosures did not stop here. To His followers He announced that the new community was to be God's light shining to the whole world. As those destined to experience the presence of God in saving activity and to manifest His power and glory, they were appointed to be the heralds of a new message which had its origin in the new covenant. Forgiveness of sins, salvation, the promised deliverance of God, now were to be proclaimed to all.

On the Stone laid in Zion the nation of Israel stumbled. Unrepentant and unmoved, they despised their king and "by wicked hands" crucified Him. Nevertheless Israel's sins could not annul God's faithfulness nor frustrate His promise of redemption. God raised His Son from the grave, and by this event proclaimed to the world that Jesus was indeed Lord and Messiah. Once more Israel was exhorted to repent and believe the Gospel. In Peter's sermons after Pentecost he addressed himself directly to the "house of Israel." "For to you is the promise, and to your children . . ." (Acts. 2:39). "Ye are the sons of the prophets, and of the covenant which God made with your fathers . . . Unto you first God, having raised up His Servant, sent him to bless you . . ." (Acts 3:25, 26). "Repent ye therefore, and turn again, that your sins may be blotted out, that so there may come seasons of refreshing from the presence of the Lord; and that he may send the Christ who hath been appointed for you, even Jesus" (Acts 3:19, 20).

The sons of the Kingdom turned away. Samaritans, proselytes, and Gentiles began to enter in, but the Jews remained unrepentant. The community of God could no longer be identified with Israel. In her place emerged a new community, constituted by Christ, that was neither Jew nor Greek, but a new creation. In this new redeemed community God now gave witness to His eternal power and glory. Through it God demonstrated His faithfulness to His promises. By it God was pleased to announce to the world His salvation.

But what of Israel? Does the creation of the new Israel of God, the church of Jesus Christ, imply that she is without hope, and that God's promises to her have become of no effect? Does this mean that God hath "cast off his people?" Paul's answer was, "God forbid . . . God did not cast off his people which he foreknew" (Rom. 11:1, 2). Israel, though indeed broken off and without part in God's visible community, yet possesses the promise (Rom. 9:4). Unrepentant Israel, provoked to jealousy by the Gentiles, shall one day repent (Rom. 11:11). This is God's covenant with His people.

For I would not, brethren, have you ignorant of this mystery, lest ye be wise in your own conceits, that a hardening in part hath befallen Israel, until the fulness of the Gentiles be come in; and so all Israel shall be saved . . . And this is my covenant unto them, when I shall take away their sins. As touching the gospel, they are enemies for your sakes; but as touching the election, they are beloved for the fathers' sake. For the gifts and calling of God are not repented of (Rom. 11:25–29).

Now if their fall is the riches of the world, and their loss the riches of the Gentiles; how much more their fulness? (Rom. 11:12)

For if the casting away of them is the reconciling of the world, what shall the receiving of them be, but life from the dead? (Rom. 11:15).

With these plain words Paul spells out the fact that God's redemptive activity will not cease until the Jewish people have resumed their place in the covenant community. This return of Israel to her God appears to constitute part of the Messianic triumph at the end of the age.

THE CHURCH AND THE BODY OF CHRIST

Perhaps nowhere did Paul experience the inadequacy of human language more than in the attempt to express the truth of God concerning the church. In a veritable maze of metaphors he describes the company of believers in such terms as "the bride of Christ," "the temple of the Holy Spirit," "the building of God," "God's husbandry." More significant, however, than any of these, and certainly more basic for general understanding, is the description of the church as the body of Christ.

It is unfortunate that some branches of Christendom have used this metaphor as an occasion for ecclesiastical self-glorying. Pressing the metaphor beyond measure, they have reduced Christ to an attribute of their own church. Making themselves identical to Christ and possessing divine rank, they have achieved a high ecclesiology at the expense of Christ. In the Roman Catholic and Greek Orthodox Churches this tendency comes to its ultimate and most pathetic expression as each asserts its claim to be uniquely and solely the body of Christ.

On the other hand, we who represent modern conservative Protestantism are not without fault. Reacting to "high churchism," many among us have frequently lost the significance of the metaphor altogether. Denying that the Lord's supper and baptism have any real relevance with respect to the body of Christ, we interpret these institutions symbolically. But insofar as the body of Christ is concerned, they have tended to become symbolic of precisely nothing. It is necessary, then, to set forth several of the more vital implications of this expression as it is used to describe the relationship of the church to Jesus Christ.

The most characteristic expression of Pauline Christianity is the formula "in Christ." Paul depends upon this unique expression 164 times to describe the intimate fellowship which a Christian has with the living Christ. Again and again "Christ in us," or "we in Christ," becomes the basis upon which Paul makes an appeal. Paul knows that no one can realize fully his existence as a Christian apart from understanding this vital union.

Union with Christ, however, is not simply a matter of a bilateral relationship between one believer and Christ. Such a possibility would have been inconceivable to Paul. It is in the church that the fullness of union with Christ is expressed. For this reason Paul says to the Corinthian church, "Now ye are the body of Christ." Without question the whole church is meant, but it is equally true that the Corinthian church and each local church in her special setting is the body of Christ.

What does it mean to be this body? It means that the church is not something dead, but because it is His body it is alive as Christ is alive. Through her veins flows the resurrection life of Christ. The power of Christ and the love of Christ fill her whole being. The church is filled by Him, loved by Him, sustained by Him. Even though the church is torn by controversy, rent by strife, and humiliated by sins, her triumph is assured as she lives in anticipation of the resurrection. Positively, it means to be so indissolubly joined to the Lord as to "become one Spirit with Him." Negatively, it means that every activity of the church and every individual member of the body is measured in terms of this union.

In the Lord's supper Paul finds the most graphic portrayal of the union. When the church receives the cup she witnesses to her *koinōnia*, her "participation" or "sharing" in Christ's blood. To "break the bread" is to witness to the participation of the church in the body of Christ. In Ephesians 5:30 (A.V.) the same thought is echoed: "For we are members of his body, of his flesh, and of his bones." When members participate in the "body and blood" of Christ (not the elements, but the life and death of Christ as it is signified by those elements (*cf.* Phil. 2:7, 8; Rom. 8:3), they participate in Christ. Thus their life and the life of the church are nourished. As the church feasts upon Him and cleaves to Him, she lives out His life and becomes His witness to the world.

In the Gospel of John this union may be recognized under still another figure, the vine and the branches. As the vine lives out its life through its branches, so Christ lives in His church. "I will come to you. . . . In that day ye will know that I am in my Father, and you in me and I in you" (John 14:18, 20 R.S.V.). As Thornton has said, "the relationship which is thus sustained is not that of a pebble in a box, but of a living branch in a living vine." [6] Without the branches the vine would bear no fruit. Without the vine the branches cannot exist. Together Christ and the church form a perfect oneness. Without Him the church is nothing; in Him the church is everything.

The name "Body of Christ," when given to the church, glorifies Christ.[7] It is a specific claim for the supremacy of Christ, not a statement offered in praise of the visible Church. The Prison Epistles present the full expression of this concept. Here Christ is referred to for the first time as the head of the body, the overlord to the church. As the Son is subordinated to the Father, so the church is always subordinate to the head. It is the sole prerogative of Christ to rule His church and to direct her according to His purpose. All things have been placed in subjection under

His feet, and He has been given to "be head over all things to the church which is his body" (Eph. 1:22, 23, *cf.* also Col. 1:18; Eph. 5:23–24; Heb. 2:8).

The headship of Christ over the church makes even more emphatic the dependence of the body upon its head. Christ alone can redeem the church. It is the head which nurtures, sanctifies, and fills the body. The Colossian church stands condemned because it does not hold fast to the head "from whom all the body, being supplied and knit together through the joints and bands, increaseth with the increase of God" (Col. 2:19). God's purpose is that the church "grow up in all things into him, who is the head, even Christ, from whom all the body . . . maketh the increase . . . unto the building up of itself in love" (Eph. 4:15, 16). The redeemed community is thus pictured as completely dependent upon the head for the grace and power which gives true growth and strength.

In certain verses the metaphor of the body of Christ draws particular attention to the relationship which exists between the members of the body. ". . . We are members one of another" (Eph. 4:25). He "gave gifts unto men . . . And he gave some to be apostles; and some, prophets; and some, evangelists; and some, pastors and teachers; for the perfecting of the saints, unto the work of ministering, unto the building up of the body of Christ . . . [growing] up in all things into him, who is the head . . . from whom all the body fitly framed and knit together through that which every joint supplieth, according to the working in due measure of each several part, maketh the increase of the body . . ." (Eph. 4:8, 11, 12, 15, 16). "For as the body is one, and hath many members, and all the members of the body, being many, are one body . . ." for we are "baptized into one body . . . and . . . drink of one Spirit" (I Cor. 12:12, 13). He planned "that there should be no schism in the body; but that the members should have the same care one for another" (I Cor. 12:25).

Paul never envisioned a Christianity in which members could be in Christ but in isolation or opposition to each other. On the contrary, because we are members of Christ, we are therefore members one of another. In this relationship with others we are confronted by certain duties, privileges, and responsibilities. Apart from sharing in the redeemed community, no believer can exist. God has given to no one member the ability to fulfill life in the body in isolation from others (I Cor. 12:14). He has rather given to every member a certain gift of grace (I Cor. 12:7ff.), and only as each member exercises his peculiar gift can the whole body move unto perfection. From the greatest to the least, from the most noble to the lowliest, each must make his unique contribution to the life and growth of the whole (I Cor. 12:23). Moreover, he needs that ministry of grace which only another member can bestow. As a result, each stands in complete dependence upon every other member, and only as he fulfills his own God-appointed ministry can the whole body of Christ, the church, prosper.

For the members of the body to be able to live in harmony and to accomplish the purpose of Christ for the body, there are two requirements. First, death must take place in each member. Only as each dies unto himself is it possible for him to come alive in Christ. To be alive in Christ is to live and to grow with that one body, to share its shame and suffering, and to grow up in perfect unity with it. Only as each realizes that when one fails the whole is hindered, that when one suffers all must grieve, that when one is honored all may rejoice, and that when one endures all become triumphant, can the body be truly one. It means that no member may live as belonging unto himself, but each must live as belonging unto Christ. If each one becomes aware of what it means to belong wholly unto Him, he will also become aware of what it means to belong wholly to His body.

Secondly, each member must be constrained by the love of Christ. Only by this means can the church realize unity in its disunity. Although there are many members, there is but one body. It is no accident that Paul's main discourse in I Corinthians 12 on the relationship which exists between the individual members of the body of Christ is followed by I Corinthians 13. "Make love your aim," says the apostle, whatever spiritual gifts you may desire (I Cor. 14:1, R.S.V.). Without love, all else is nothing; "I am nothing . . . I gain nothing" (I Cor. 13:2, 3, R.S.V.). It is the love of Christ constraining each member that brings the body into the unity of faith and creates a perfect man.

THE CHURCH AND THE HOLY SPIRIT

It was suggested earlier that there can be no true understanding of the church of the New Testament apart from the realization that the new community has a definite continuity with the past. It is more important, however, to recognize that the community of God was completely transformed by the coming of Christ. This was the decisive event of revelation which forever separated the new community from the old. In the words of Jesus, it was the new wine that could not be poured into old wineskins. The transformation which provided the living link between the promises of God and their fulfillment in the new community was effected by the coming of the Holy Spirit. The transition between Israel and the church had not been understood clearly by the disciples of Christ.

In order to develop a sufficient grasp of this situation, it is necessary to recapitulate the circumstances leading up to it. Only after much misunderstanding on their part had God been able to reveal to the disciples that the humble and lowly Jesus of Nazareth was the promised Messiah. So fixed had become the expectation of a mighty and exalted deliverer, and so persistent was the expectation for a terrestrial kingdom, that the passion and death of Christ actually served to shatter the initial faith of the disciples. Only the appearance of the risen Christ sufficed to restore their confidence. With the re-establishment of faith, the anticipation of an earthly theocracy became even stronger. The question of the disciples recorded in Acts 1:6, "Dost thou at this time restore the kingdom to Israel?" indicates this hope. The ascension, however, decreeing the end of the physical presence of Jesus, may have placed this whole expectation in doubt.

The fulfillment of Christ's promise of the Holy Spirit provided the means for removing all this confusion. In the experience of Pentecost the disciples realized that they had been reconstituted as the redeemed community of promise. God had fulfilled the hope of Israel. Only because Jesus had been exalted at the right hand of the Father, had He been able to send forth the Spirit according to His own promise. Thus God Himself declared by the resurrection and ascension that Jesus was both Lord and Christ, the Son of God with power (Acts 2:36; Rom. 1:4).

In the death and resurrection of Christ the remission of sins had been accomplished (Acts 2:36; 5:31). Salvation was now a reality (Acts 2:38); the new covenant, the new theocracy foretold by Jeremiah and Joel, was now in full effect (Acts 2:16; 3:24). Realization of these facts brought decisive changes in the understanding of the disciples. One of these was the recognition that there were two advents, between which intervened the time of the new community of the redeemed. The divine timetable now was made clear. First, there had been the time of the past age, the time of Israel. Next was the climactic revelation of God in the earthly ministry and passion of Jesus, culminating in the resurrection. This introduced the present age marked by the Messianic exaltation of Jesus, who now reigned in heaven at God's right hand, and on earth through His Spirit in the community of the redeemed. Finally would be the restitution of all things, when Jesus Christ would appear in His glory. All things would then become subject to Him, and He would reign until every knee should bow and every tongue should confess Him as Lord. Then would come the end, when the kingdom of the Son would be delivered up to the Father.

Insofar as Christ was now seated victoriously at God's right hand, the decisive victory over sin and death had been won. Judgment now had passed into the hands of the Lord Christ. Henceforth the disciples would believe through Him, pray through Him, preach through Him, live through Him. Moreover, the presence of the Spirit gave assurance that Christ was Himself present in the midst of His followers. "We know that he abideth in us, by the Spirit which he gave us" (I John 3:24; cf. I John 4:13). To the extent that He was present through His Holy Spirit the promises made to Israel of old (Acts 2:39), to Abraham (Acts 3:25), to Moses (Acts 7:17), to David (Acts 13:33), and to all the prophets (Acts 10:43) were being fulfilled. The Messianic community of the new covenant was now in operation.

The means of entrance into this community of the redeemed is the possession of the Holy Spirit. The believers on the day of Pentecost were all filled with the Spirit; there was no distinction between male and female, between young men or old, between slaves and freemen. Receiving the Spirit brings the assurance that sins have been forgiven and that salvation has been received. It is the inward reality which corresponds to the outer symbolism of baptism, and is the supreme proof of belonging to Christ (Rom. 8:9).

Though everyone receives the Holy Spirit individually, the fact still remains that the Spirit is in a unique sense the possession of the community. This fact differentiates the New Testament community from the Old, where the Spirit was bestowed only on particular individuals for specific occasions.

The essence of the existence of the church is life in the Spirit. "The Kingdom of God is not in word but in power," Paul writes to the Corinthians (I Cor. 4:20). The preaching of the disciples is "not in persuasive words of wisdom, but in demonstration of the Spirit and of power" (I Cor. 2:4). The Galatians' experience of the ministration of the Spirit in miracles and gifts (Gal. 3:5) led Paul to conclude: "Since we live in the Spirit, let us also walk in the Spirit" (Gal. 5:25). The Spirit empowers the church (Acts 1, 2), accompanies the witness of the disciples (Acts 5:32), and directs their missionary work (Acts 8:29; 10:19–20; 13:2; 16:6–8). The united possession of the Holy Spirit explains the "togetherness" which the church experienced, the willingness to have all things in common, the bond of fellowship which marked their gathering. They could not be other than one in the Lord.

The implications of this power of the Spirit are incalculable. The early church possessed a dynamic directly from

God which resulted in the conversion of souls, the opening of prison doors, the judgment of sin within the church, the ability to withstand opposition and persecution; a dynamic, in short, which the gates of hell could not withstand. Sadly enough, this dynamic is missing in great measure from our churches today. As Brunner expresses it, "In any event, we ought to face the New Testament witness with sufficient candour to admit that in this 'pneuma,' which the *ekklesia* was conscious of possessing, there lie forces of an extrarational kind which are mostly lacking among us Christians of today." [8]

The Holy Spirit's relation to the Church was not simply an external power coming from without, "shaking" or filling the church. The Spirit baptized every member of the church, with the result that each one became specifically endowed or equipped to perform special service. As Paul states to the Corinthians: "To each one is given the manifestation of the Spirit to profit withal" (I Cor. 12:7); to one is given a "word of wisdom; and to another the word of knowledge . . . to another faith . . . to another prophecy . . . but all these worketh the one and the same Spirit, dividing to each one severally even as he will" (I Cor. 12:8–11). "But unto each one of us was the grace given according to the measure of the gift of Christ . . . for the perfecting of the saints, unto the work of ministering, unto the building up of the body of Christ" (Eph. 4:7–12).

The gifts of the Spirit are a direct challenge to the ecclesiastical temper of our day with its distinction between clergy and laity, as if the clergy possessed the gifts of God and the laity depended upon their administration of the gifts. Rather, all are members in the same body, irrespective of what official capacity they may or may not be called to fill. *All* members are called to minister to the body "till *all* attain unto the unity of the faith, and of the knowledge of the Son of God, unto a fullgrown man, unto the measure of the stature of the fullness of Christ" (Eph. 4:13). Through the recognition and exercise of these individual endowments the human tendency toward separation within the body of Christ is overcome. Because each possesses a full share of the Holy Spirit, and because each in turn is directed by the Holy Spirit according to His apportionment, envy, malice, or jealousy need not and should not exist. He who has received the Holy Spirit will walk in the confidence of His love, will speak in love, and will submit to another for Christ's sake. Only where this mutual subordination exists, and where the church, in turn, is subject to Christ, can the Holy Spirit "fill" the church and make manifest the unity of the Body of Christ.

SEVEN

CHRISTIAN ETHICS

V. RAYMOND EDMAN

Dr. V. Raymond Edman joined the faculty of Wheaton College in 1936 as a member of the Department of History after service on the mission field in Ecuador and in a pastorate. In the following year he became chairman of the department. In 1940 he was made acting President of the college, and President in 1941. He is a graduate of Boston University (A.B.), Clark University (A.M., Ph.D.), and holds honorary degrees of LL.D. from Houghton College, and D.D. from Taylor University. He is widely known as a conference speaker, and has written a history of missions, The Light in Dark Ages (1949), *and numerous devotional works, among the best known of which are* The Disciplines of Life (1948) *and* The Delights of Life (1954).

Any religion worthy of consideration contains ethical content and implications. That is especially true of Christianity, which is confident that it is based on revelation from Almighty God, and is not merely the result of human thought and reflection. By and large the Old Testament gives the letter of ethical principles and the New Testament elaborates the spirit thereof.

Irreligion and atheism are intrinsically non-ethical. In the *Communist Manifesto*, Karl Marx declared: "Law, morality, religion, are . . . . so many bourgeois prejudices, behind which lurk in ambush just as many bourgeois interests." Lenin, in a message given at the Third All-Russian Congress of the Young Communist League of the Soviet Union (October 2, 1920), stated specifically: [1]

In what sense do we deny ethics, morals?

In the sense in which they are preached by the bourgeoisie, which deduces these morals from god's commandments. Of course, we say that we do not believe in god. We know perfectly well that the clergy, the landlords, and the bourgeoisie all claim to speak in the name of god, in order to protect their own interests as exploiters. Or, instead of deducing their ethics from the commandments of morality, from the commandments of god, they deduce them from idealistic or semi-idealistic phrases which in substance were always very similar to divine commandments.

We deny all morality taken from superhuman or non-class conceptions. We say that this is a deception, a swindle, a befogging of the minds of the workers and peasants in the interests of the landlords and capitalists.

We say that our morality is wholly subordinated to the interests of the class struggle of the proletariat. We deduce our morality from the facts and needs of the class struggle of the proletariat. . . .

That is why we say that a morality taken from outside of human society does not exist for us; it is a fraud. For us morality is subordinated to the interests of the proletarian class struggle. . . .

When God is banished from human concept and conviction, ethics and morality become non-existent or are wholly relative and defined according to one's own terms and conduct. The old proverb, "There is honor among thieves," has some ethical content; but even this seems to be wholly absent in Communism, where suspicion, deceit, double-dealing, and death are major factors in the struggle for pre-eminence and power.

Likewise, when men make gods in their own image, imaginary deities that are in reality the lengthened shadow of man, ethics and morality are at best uncertain, indefinite, and usually relative. The measuring stick for morality is too short for true value judgment.

In the midst of mid-twentieth-century resurgence of old materialism with its relativistic morality, if any, there is need for reaffirmation of Christian ethical standards and rededication thereto. In the moral chaos of this day when ethics is considered, if at all, apart from any standards of fixed value, there is urgent call that someone proclaim, like the prophets of old, "Thus saith the Lord"!

Ethics is generally regarded as the science of moral duty which is designed to determine the ideal human character and the ideal end of human action. Usually it is synonymous with morality, although ethics should relate to inner motivation as well as to outward manner of life. For our purpose we differentiate Christian ethics from general ethics. The latter is the result of human thought and reflection over the centuries in man's search for the good life. Much of general ethics is commendable and constructive, and some of it compares very favorably with Christian ethics based upon divine revelation. Keyser presents an adequate definition in saying, "Christian Ethics is the science which treats of the sources, principles and practice of right and wrong in the light of the Holy Scriptures, in addition to the light of nature and reason." [2]

The good life has always been the goal of some of mankind. Thoughtful men have reflected on morality and made judgment on human conduct, their own and that of others. They have sought to captivate the inner disposition and to control the outward activity of life which make for the highest good, *summum bonum.* The right motivation should result in the correct manner of life and give true meaning to it. For mankind, however, ethics has continued to be a difficult search, a distant goal. Even after much philosophic search mankind has been left with wistful, wishful thinking about the good life, or with wicked, embittered cynicism.

As an area of human thought, ethics, like all other subjects of philosophic contemplation, has been basically materialistic or idealistic, dependent upon one's view of the universe and man's place therein. Materialists differ among themselves as to details, from the early Sophists like Protagoras and the Cynics of Ancient Greece to moderns like John Dewey and Bertrand Russell. The list of materialists is long and formidable; but despite divergence in details, among them nature is the ultimate reality and man is limited to the knowledge of himself and his own feelings. Stoic and Epicurean, Utilitarian and Marxist, Pragmatist and Positivist, gentle scholar like Spinoza or tough-minded realist like Machiavelli, all are in basic agreement that man is the measure of all things. "Virtue is knowledge and ignorance is vice," taught Socrates; but neither he nor materialists since him have found that self-knowledge means that man is intrinsically and naturally inclined to the good.

The effect of naturalism on human thought and conduct over the centuries has been well summarized by Henry in his *Christian Personal Ethics:* [3]

Naturalism can neither explain human life, and its moral claim, nor ennoble it. It inculcates inevitably a complacency towards moral evil. The more consistent its revolt against truth and morality, and against the supernatural spiritual world, the more it seeks not only to justify sin, but to hallow its manifestations, until at last it ventures a scheme of life predicated upon counter-morality. Some followers of Naturalism may revolt against objective morality and yet retain some of its elements for prudential reasons; others may discard the whole, yet halt short of Nietzsche's lust for power. Thoroughgoing Naturalism, however, uncontained by factors of sentiment and prudence, leads to sheer immoralism which rises from the disturbing recognition that, if space-time nature constitutes the whole of reality, the moral imperative is but an arbitrary and external imposition upon the changing movements of reality. The long sweep of naturalistic ethics has coalesced to encourage widespread unbelief in objective standards. For that reason vast multitudes have had only the feeblest standards to invoke, to resist or to challenge those aggressive forces of totalitarianism, which seek by sheer violence to enforce their arbitrary external claims. The much-publicized "strength and maturity" of disbelief in changeless moral distinctions at last exacts as its costly toll man's own weak inability, especially in a tired age which lacks faith in anything eternal, to defy the arbitrary imposition of an ethics sanctioned only by might.

Idealism is at the same time a protest against materialism and an aspiration for something beyond the immediate and the material. Socrates placed man in nature; Plato saw him in the cosmos. Man is more than an animal, and is related to a spiritual, supernatural realm. Reality is more than space and time. Truth and morality are more than custom and convention. Beyond the world of sight and sense there is spiritual reality, of which man is but a fragment.

Idealists, like materialists, differ decidedly among themselves as to details; but their basic persuasion is the same. Plato and Aristotle, Kant and Hegel, Hocking and Kierkegaard, by knowledge, by dialectics, by categorical imperative, and by existentialism have sought to make mankind a part of divine Reason, to make virtue a habit, and to relate mortal man with transcendent deity.

Idealism is a very commendable search for understanding and reality. With the lamp of reason it takes the high road above the miasma of materialism. Reason is self-sufficient to trace out eternal truth and its ethical implications. Ethical norms are autonomous and rise from within the individual. Reason has therefore no need for revelation and is constitutionally opposed thereto. Christianity with its dependence upon revelation and redemption is anathema to the completely consistent idealist.

CHRISTIAN ETHICS

Christian ethics as a branch of general ethics is based squarely on the Bible as the revelation of Almighty God. Instead of constituting a long and painful search after right motivation and manner of life, Scriptural ethics is in reality the result of God's search after mankind. The Bible does not portray man as reaching upward and outward for God; contrariwise, it shows that the Almighty has sought after man from the very outset of human history. By angel and prophet, by law and literature, the Most High sought to teach men in Old Testament times and to bring them to uprightness of life and fellowship with Himself.

Revelation through prophets and poets of Israel continued through Malachi. After a silence of four centuries it was resumed in the coming of the Saviour and in the teaching of the apostles under inspiration of the Holy Spirit. Whether history or prophecy, commandment or poetry, biography or epistle, the sacred Scriptures present the divine ethical standards established by the Almighty.

Biblical ethics based upon revelation stresses the value of

the human soul. Man is the direct handiwork of the Almighty, created in the image of God. Placed in the earth he was given magnificent opportunity to exercise all his God-given principles and prerogatives. As a created being man was responsible to the Ethical Being and, of necessity, to other ethical human beings who would be in the world.

By the Fall the image of God was marred, defaced, distorted, but not entirely destroyed. Through the universe about him man was aware of a divine Creator; but he preferred to follow his own inclination toward sinfulness and to formulate his own religions. Paul describes vividly the discordant, disobedient soul of man:

Because that which may be known of God is manifest in them; for God hath shewed it unto them. For the invisible things of him from the creation of the world are clearly seen, being understood by the things that are made, even his eternal power and Godhead; so that they are without excuse: because that, when they knew God, they glorified him not as God, neither were thankful; but became vain in their imaginations, and their foolish heart was darkened. Professing themselves to be wise, they became fools, and changed the glory of the uncorruptible God into an image made like to corruptible man, and to birds, and four-footed beasts, and creeping things (Rom. 1:19-23).

For right ethical principles and performance man needed a new revelation by word that would be more explicit and exacting than that which could be derived from the works of the Creator. Likewise, he needed a new nature so that he might live according to the light given in that Word.

The standards of ethical character and conduct established in the Scriptures are stated in various ways. On occasion these are given by explicit mandate, as in the Decalogue. Again, they may be illustrated in the historical record.

Monogamy is implied in the original institution of marriage as stated in Genesis 2:24 — "Therefore shall a man leave his father and his mother, and shall cleave unto his wife: and they shall be one flesh." The standard of chastity is recorded in the first reference to Rebecca (Gen. 24:16). Envy and hatred are shown in their true light in the account of Cain and Abel (Gen. 4:1–15).

Furthermore, ethical principles were enforced pointedly by the prophets in their denunciation of personal and national wickedness, while the poets in the Psalms and the Proverbs taught moral standards in the lilt of song and the wisdom of Solomon. From the first pages of Genesis to the closing chapters of Revelation the Bible sets forth the ethical standards established by the Most High.

The most concise statement of Old Testament ethics is to be found in the law of Moses, with its Ten Commandments and its regulations for the individual, the family, and the nation. Stern as was the law, it was the expression of divine standards of righteousness, and yet it provided care for the poor, for slaves, aliens, and animals. The law was preparatory for the gospel, as Paul declares, "the schoolmaster to bring us unto Christ" (Gal. 3:24). It contained the clear letter of divine regulation and requirements. While largely external and taken up primarily with the material, it provided a standard more explicit and detailed than any devised by philosophers of antiquity.

Urgent was the Old Testament emphasis upon ethical conduct, as evidenced in the prophetic cry of Isaiah:

Wash you, make you clean; put away the evil of your doings from before mine eyes; cease to do evil; learn to do well; seek judgment, relieve the oppressed, judge the fatherless, plead for the widow. Come now, and let us reason together, saith the Lord: though your sins be as scarlet, they shall be as white as snow; though they be red like crimson, they shall be as wool (Isa. 1:16–18).

The ethical message of the Old Testament is well epitomized in the comprehensive statement of Micah 6:8 — "He hath shewed thee, O man, what is good; and what doth the Lord require of thee, but to do justly, and to love mercy, and to walk humbly with thy God?" (Micah 6:8).

The book of Proverbs is another Old Testament portion especially pertinent in the area of ethics. It concerns itself, to be sure, more with outward conduct than with inner dynamic; nevertheless, it constitutes one of the finest statements of morality to be found in any source, sacred or profane. Virtues are exalted and made emphatic, while vices are portrayed in their true light. Humility, honesty, unselfishness, teachableness, detachment from evil and attachment to the good, reverence for parents and loyalty to friends, integrity, chastity, industriousness are taught by precept and are enjoined to practice. The "happy man" with the good life is the "wise man" of Proverbs who knows right standards and conscientiously lives by them. The "foolish man" in Proverbs is not unintelligent, ignorant, or mentally deficient; rather, he is arrogant, self-sufficient, selfish, and essentially godless.

New Testament ethics is summarized primarily in the Sermon on the Mount, which is the Saviour's commentary on the law given at Sinai. The truly happy ones are not the proud, the gay and unconcerned, the wealthy, and the prominent. Rather, blessed are the humble, the "poor in spirit" (Matt. 5:3–7), as are the mourners, the meek, and the merciful. Likewise happy are the pure in heart, the peacemakers, and those persecuted for their upright manner of life. The law is not letter only, but also spirit. Hatred is murder, lust is adultery. Marriage is a sacred obligation, and divorce is allowed only under particular conditions, and that "because of the hardness of your hearts." Affection and consideration are due one's enemies as well as one's friends, "That ye may be the children of your Father which is in heaven: for he maketh his sun to rise on the evil and on the good, and sendeth rain on the just and on the unjust" (Matt. 5:45).

The ethical persuasion and the moral practice presented by the New Testament are made possible by two basic factors: regeneration and instruction, both by the Holy Spirit. "Ye must be born again," the Saviour stated specifically. "All have sinned and come short of the glory of God; being justified freely by his grace through the redemption that is in Christ Jesus," elaborated the Apostle Paul (Rom. 3:23, 24). The image of the Almighty, defaced and debased in man by the Fall, must be restored. Man's sinfulness must be forgiven, his waywardness checked, his rebellion come to an end. His ignorance of the true God is dispelled by the Bible which becomes "a lamp to his feet and a light to his path." Spiritually dead in trespasses and sins, he is made alive by the impartation of divine life through the Holy Spirit. By God's salvation he is released from the penalty of past sin and finds provision for victorious living over present sins. In the cogent summary of II Corinthians 5:17: "If any man be in Christ, he is a new creature: old things are passed away; behold, all things are become new."

For the Christian, morality proceeds from within and is not merely a cloak put on the outside. There is inner motivation to right conduct because of the new life principle. Paul reminded the Corinthian Christians that some of them had been thieves, covetous, drunkards, revilers, extortioners, immoral, idolaters, saying, "And such were some of you: but ye are washed, but ye are sanctified, but ye are justified in the name of the Lord Jesus, and by the Spirit of our God" (I Cor. 6:11).

The new life principle and the inner motivation to righteousness of conduct are not without conflict in the life of the Christian. Stated the observant Paul, writing by inspiration of the Holy Spirit, "Walk in the Spirit, and ye shall not fulfil the lust of the flesh. For the flesh lusteth against the Spirit, and the Spirit against the flesh: and these are contrary the one to the other: so that ye cannot do the things that ye would. But if ye be led of the Spirit, ye are not under the law" (Gal. 5:16-18).

Instruction in ethical principles and practice is necessary for the Christian. As will be noted later, the teachings of Jesus are filled with ethical content. The letters of Paul contain usually a doctrinal introduction followed by explicit ethical instruction. The letter to the Ephesian Christians, for example, states in the first three chapters the believer's relationship to the Almighty by faith, and then proceeds in the remaining three chapters to make application of that relationship to the attitude and action of the individual Christian. Humility, compassion for others, honesty, holiness, truthfulness, patience, integrity, kindness, freedom from such vices as bitterness and wrath and evil speaking, submissiveness of husbands and wives one to another, and reverence of children to their parents are among the virtues enjoined in the epistle.

By Christian instruction the conscience is enlightened and made sensitive to divine standards. Conscience is made teachable and tender, and becomes truly the guiding principle of the good life. It becomes the compass of moral conduct, steering the life by standards outside mankind. It gives perspective and persuasion as to divine principles, much as the ship's captain steers by the long perspective of the compass and the stars and not by some detail of his ship or the passing emotions of the moment. The compass of conscience causes one to steer steadily through sunshine of prosperity and storms of adversity and temptation.

Because conscience is instructed, convictions are deepened and become a part of life's pattern. The Christian is to be a "doer of the word, and not a hearer only." Declared the Lord Jesus, "If ye know these things, happy are ye if ye do them." True contentment of the good life comes from doing what is right as well as from knowing it.

Christian conduct therefore is to be careful, cautious, consistent and Christlike. It is to be marked by a growth into maturity, and not to remain always in the stage of childishness. "Be ye perfect even as your Father in heaven is perfect," admonished Jesus in the Sermon on the Mount (Matt. 5:48). Added Paul, "Till we all come in the unity of the faith, and of the knowledge of the Son of God, unto a perfect man, unto the measure of the stature of the fulness of Christ: that we henceforth be no more children, tossed to and fro . . . but speaking the truth in love, may grow up into him in all things, which is the head, even Christ" (Eph. 4:13–15).

THE ETHICS OF THE LORD JESUS

The ethical teaching of the Saviour was given not in profound philosophical propositions, but in the naturalness and simplicity of everyday life. The thinkers of antiquity before him had made attempts to enumerate the virtues but had found considerable difficulty in so doing. Plato's list is meager at best, and that of Aristotle is neither systematic nor complete. In no one place did the Lord Jesus make a category of ethical precepts; but as one makes a subject list of His teachings he finds the breadth and depth of divine statement on ethics.

The summary of the Saviour's teaching is epitomized in His response to the inquiry: "What is the great commandment?" In His reply (Matt. 22:36–40) the Master brought together two commandments widely separated in the Old Testament canon. "Thou shalt love the Lord thy God with all thy heart, and with all thy soul, and with all thy mind. This is the first and great commandment (Deut. 6:5). And the second is like unto it, thou shalt love thy neighbor as thyself. On these two commandments hang all the law and prophets" (Lev. 19:18).

These two basic requirements — supreme love to the Almighty and selfless love for one's fellow man — constitute the substance of the Decalogue, whose first four commandments refer to our relationship with God and the latter six with our neighbor. These concepts are not considered adequately, if at all, in non-Christian philosophies, and nowhere do we find them joined together except in the teaching of Jesus.

True worship must be intrinsically spiritual, taught the Saviour. "But the hour cometh, and now is, when the true worshippers shall worship the Father in spirit and in truth: for the Father seeketh such to worship him. God is a Spirit: and they that worship him must worship him in spirit and in truth" (John 4:23–24).

The kingdom of God is to be foremost in human consideration, even as the Master declared, "Seek ye first the kingdom of God, and his righteousness; and all these things shall be added unto you" (Matt. 6:33). This kingdom is entered by the process of regeneration and is not the prerogative of human race or religion. In His reply to Nicodemus, the Teacher stated specifically: "Verily, verily, I say unto thee, Except a man be born again, he cannot see the kingdom of God. . . . That which is born of the flesh is flesh; and that which is born of the Spirit is spirit. Marvel not that I said unto thee, Ye must be born again" (John 3:3, 6, 7).

The members of that kingdom are to be "the salt of the earth" and the "light of the world" (Matt. 5:13–16). Life is to be so consistent with godliness that others are to see "your good works, and glorify your Father which is in heaven." Any difficulty between fellow men breaks off fellowship with God and true worship. Reconciliation with another, even with one's adversary, is to be made before there is true worship.

Humility is a hallmark of the true Christian. "Take my yoke upon you, and learn of me; for I am meek and lowly in heart: and ye shall find rest unto your souls" (Matt. 11:29). As evidence thereof one is taught not to seek preferment of any kind; rather, to take the lowest place from which one can be called to a higher. Love for one's fellow men was spelled out in the golden rule: "Therefore all things whatsoever ye would that men should do to you, do ye even so to them: for this is the law and the prophets" (Matt. 7:12). The Lord elaborated that truth in making it to be a new commandment by which His disciples would be known. "A new commandment I give unto you, That ye love one another; as I have loved you, that ye also love one another. By this shall all men know that ye are my disciples, if ye have love one to another" (John 13:34–35).

Jesus taught that such consideration and concern should extend to one's enemies as well as to one's friends. "But I say unto you which hear, Love your enemies, do good to them which hate you, bless them that curse you, and pray for them which despitefully use you. . . . For if ye love them which love you, what thank have ye? for sinners also love those that love them. And if ye do good to them which do good to you, what thank have ye? for sinners also do even the same. And if ye lend to them of whom ye hope to receive, what thank have ye? for sinners also lend to sinners, to receive as much again. But love ye your enemies, and do good, and lend, hoping for nothing again; and your reward shall be great, and ye shall be the children of the Highest: for he is kind unto the unthankful and to the evil" (Luke 6:27-28, 32-35).

Unselfish thoughtfulness for others was likewise basic. "Give, and it shall be given unto you; good measure, pressed down, and shaken together, and running over, shall men give into your bosom. For with the same measure that ye mete withal it shall be measured to you again" (Luke 6:38). With this was coupled the warning not to be ostentatious in one's giving. "Take heed that ye do not your alms before men, to be seen of them: otherwise ye have no reward of your Father which is in heaven. Therefore when thou doest thine alms, do not sound a trumpet before thee, as the hypocrites do in the synagogues and in the streets, that they may have glory of men. Verily I say unto you, They have their reward. But when thou doest alms, let not thy left hand know what thy right hand doeth: that thine alms may be in secret: and thy Father which seeth in secret himself shall reward thee openly" (Matt. 6:1-4).

Likewise, one is not to have concern only for those who can return in kind; rather, compassion and provision should be for the most needy. The Saviour said: "Then said he also to him that bade him, When thou makest a dinner or a supper, call not thy friends, nor thy brethren, neither thy kinsmen, nor thy rich neighbours; lest they also bid thee again, and a recompence be made thee. But when thou makest a feast, call the poor, the maimed, the lame, the blind: and thou shalt be blessed; for they cannot recompense thee: for thou shall be recompensed at the resurrection of the just" (Luke 14:12–14).

The spirit of forgiveness toward others was frequently stressed. "Forgive, and ye shall be forgiven" (Luke 6:37). He added: "And when ye stand praying, forgive, if ye have ought against any: that your Father also which is in heaven may forgive your trespasses. But if ye do not forgive, neither will your Father which is in heaven forgive your trespasses" (Mark 11: 25–26). He himself gave us the greatest example of forgiveness when on the cross He prayed, "Father, forgive them; for they know not what they do" (Luke 23:34).

Self-renunciation was frequently emphasized by the Master. "Then said Jesus unto his disciples, If any man will come after me, let him deny himself, and take up his cross, and follow me. For whosoever will save his life shall lose it: and whosoever will lose his life for my sake shall find it. For what is a man profited, if he shall gain the whole world, and lose his own soul? or what shall a man give in exchange for his soul?" (Matt. 16:24–26).

Jesus said that purity of life was essential. "Blessed are the pure in heart: for they shall see God" (Matt. 5:8). He showed that the inner motivation was the source of good or evil. "A good man out of the good treasure of his heart bringeth forth that which is good; and an evil man out of the evil treasure of his heart bringeth forth that which is evil: for of the abundance of the heart his mouth speaketh" (Luke 6:45). To this He added the necessity for uprightness of speech: "I say unto you, That every idle word that men shall speak, they shall give account thereof in the day of judgment" (Matt. 12:36).

Faithfulness was frequently enjoined in our Lord's teaching. "He that is faithful in that which is least is faithful also in much: and he that is unjust in the least is unjust also in much" (Luke 16:10). "Who then is a faithful and wise servant, whom his lord hath made ruler over his household, to give them meat in due season? Blessed is that servant, whom his lord when he cometh shall find so doing. Verily I say unto you, That he shall make him ruler over all his goods" (Matt. 24:45–47). To the diligent and dependable was the assurance given that there would be recompense and recognition: "Well done, thou good and faithful servant: thou hast been faithful over a few things, I will make thee ruler over many things: enter thou into the joy of thy lord" (Matt. 25:21).

Steadfastness, perseverance, and patience are truly Christian virtues. The Saviour gave the warning, "No man, having put his hand to the plow, and looking back, is fit for the kingdom of God" (Luke 9:62). Likewise He taught: "If ye continue in my word, then are ye my disciples indeed; and ye shall know the truth, and the truth shall make you free" (John 8:31–32). "In your patience," He stated, "possess ye your souls" (Luke 21:19).

The true spirit of the Christian is one of unselfish service rather than self-seeking. When Jesus gave the supreme example, washing His disciples' feet, He declared, "Know ye what I have done to you? Ye call me Master and Lord: and ye say well; for so I am. If I then, your Lord and Master, have washed your feet; ye also ought to wash one another's feet. For I have given you an example, that ye should do as I have done to you. Verily, verily, I say unto you, The servant is not greater than his lord; neither he that is sent greater than he that sent him. If ye know these things, happy are ye if ye do them" (John 13:12–17).

He taught the faith in the Almighty which brings freedom

from anxiety and worry. That profound truth He stated in the simplest of terms in the sermon on the mount: "Therefore I say unto you, Take no thought for your life, what ye shall eat, or what ye shall drink; nor yet for your body, what ye shall put on. Is not the life more than meat, and the body than raiment? Behold the fowls of the air: for they sow not, neither do they reap, nor gather into barns; yet your heavenly Father feedeth them. Are ye not much better than they? Which of you by taking thought can add one cubit unto his stature? And why take ye thought for raiment? Consider the lilies of the field, how they grow; they toil not, neither do they spin: and yet I say unto you, That even Solomon in all his glory was not arrayed like one of these. Wherefore, if God so clothe the grass of the field, which today is, and tomorrow is cast into the oven, shall he not much more clothe you, O ye of little faith?" (Matt. 6:25–30).

Closely allied to trust in God He taught thankfulness toward the Most High and toward one's fellows. To the cleansed leper He said simply, "See thou tell no man; but go thy way, shew thyself to the priest, and offer the gift that Moses commanded, for a testimony unto them" (Matt. 8:4). When ten were cleansed, He was surprised that only one returned to express gratitude.

The Saviour's teaching contained many warnings against unethical attitude and action. Hypocrisy He could not tolerate. Pointedly did He preach to the hypocrites of His day: "But woe unto you, scribes and Pharisees, hypocrites! for ye shut up the kingdom of heaven against men: for ye neither go in yourselves, neither suffer ye them that are entering to go in. Woe unto you, scribes and Pharisees, hypocrites! for ye devour widows' houses, and for a pretence make long prayer: therefore ye shall receive the greater damnation. . . . Woe unto you, scribes and Pharisees, hypocrites! for ye make clean the outside of the cup and of the platter, but within they are full of extortion and excess" (Matt. 23:13–14, 25).

Likewise He spoke out against pride saying, "For whosoever exalteth himself shall be abased; and he that humbleth himself shall be exalted" (Luke 14:11).

"Beware of covetousness," He stated often, adding, "for a man's life consisteth not in the abundance of the things which he possesseth" (Luke 12:15). Covetousness proceeds from within, "out of the heart of men" (Mark 7:21–22).

Gently did He rebuke Martha for her undue concern about material considerations. "Martha, Martha, thou art careful and troubled about many things: but one thing is needful: and Mary hath chosen that good part, which shall not be taken away from her" (Luke 10:41–42). To those tempted by material goods He explained: "Lay not up for yourselves treasures upon earth, where moth and rust doth corrupt, and where thieves break through and steal: but lay up for yourselves treasures in heaven, where neither moth nor rust doth corrupt, and where thieves do not break through nor steal: for where your treasure is, there will your heart be also" (Matt. 6:19–21).

Graphically He explained the sin of judging the motives and actions of another. "Judge not, that ye be not judged. For with what judgment ye judge, ye shall be judged: and with what measure ye mete, it shall be measured to you again. And why beholdest thou the mote that is in thy brother's eye, but considerest not the beam that is in thine own eye? Or how wilt thou say to thy brother, Let me pull out the mote out of thine eye; and, behold, a beam is in thine own eye? Thou hypocrite, first cast out the beam out of thine own eye; and then shalt thou see clearly to cast out the mote out of thy brother's eye" (Matt. 7:1–5).

Inconsistency with one's profession of godliness was given

earnest warning. It were better that one be drowned in the depth of the sea, He taught, than to cause "one of these little ones which believe in me" to stumble. "Take heed that ye despise not one of these little ones; for I say unto you, That in heaven their angels do always behold the face of my Father which is in heaven" (Matt. 18:6, 10). Of little ones declared the tender Teacher: "Suffer little children, and forbid them not, to come unto me: for of such is the kingdom of heaven" (Matt. 19:14).

Everywhere in His teaching the Lord Jesus taught human accountability to Almighty God and to one's fellow men in this life and in the future righteous judgment of God. Accountability to the Creator is undoubtedly one of the strongest incentives to ethical attitude and moral conduct.

Likewise, throughout His ministry the Lord Jesus emphasized human inability to achieve the standards set down by the Almighty, but gave promise that the new life imparted in regeneration and the infilling of the Holy Spirit could and should achieve these objectives. The truly Christian life proceeds from within outward, and not the reverse. Taught the Saviour: "Abide in me, and I in you. As the branch cannot bear fruit of itself, except it abide in the vine; no more can ye except ye abide in me. I am the vine, ye are the branches: He that abideth in me, and I in him, the same bringeth forth much fruit: for without me ye can do nothing" (John 15:4–5). The Apostle Paul developed that teaching: "But the fruit of the Spirit is love, joy, peace, longsuffering, gentleness, goodness, faith, meekness, temperance: against such there is no law. And they that are Christ's have crucified the flesh with the affections and lusts. If we live in the Spirit, let us also walk in the Spirit" (Gal. 5:22–25).

In his second epistle (II Pet. 1:3–8) Peter made further

elaboration of the Christian life: "According as his divine power hath given unto us all things that pertain unto life and godliness, through the knowledge of him that hath called us to glory and virtue: whereby are given unto us exceeding great and precious promises: that by these ye might be partakers of the divine nature, having escaped the corruption that is in the world through lust. And beside this, giving all diligence, add to your faith virtue; and to virtue knowledge; and to knowledge temperance; and to temperance patience; and to patience godliness; and to godliness brotherly kindness; and to brotherly kindness charity. For if these things be in you, and abound, they make you that ye shall neither be barren nor unfruitful in the knowledge of our Lord Jesus Christ."

The ethical teachings of the Lord Jesus were understood and taught by His followers. The New Testament epistles contained many practical admonitions and explanations on true worship, love, humility, charity, forgiveness, self-renunciation, faithfulness, steadfastness, and patience; along with warnings against inconsistency, indifference, judging, dishonesty, untruthfulness, and the like.

The Holy Scriptures do not profess to give a systematic philosophy of ethics and morals. They present mankind's waywardness and intrinsic wickedness and, more important, God's redemption, regeneration for the sinner, and requirements for rectitude. The ethical principles of the Scriptures call for conformity of life to the pattern laid down therein. We are to judge our life by the light of the Scriptures, for they contain God's standards of righteous living.

Conformity to Scriptural standards should lead to holiness of life and a consistency that is Christlike. Inward consecration to the Lord God should lead to outward conduct that is loving and lovely.

Christian ethics as stated in the Scriptures are absolute, making supreme claim to their authority and to our obedience. Likewise they claim universality, since they apply without exception to all mankind.

History now knows virtue, for it has seen Christ. Christian morality is nothing more than Jesus Christ in his followers. They live as he lived, for he now lives in them. The Christian system of morality can be summed up in the person of Christ. For what the Christian means by a virtuous life is really Jesus Christ, as the incomparable example of the Divine ideal realized in the flesh. It is not too much to say that for Christian ethics, virtue is identical with the rectitude and purity of Jesus Christ. What Christianity acquired from Jesus Christ was not merely a widening of the universal scope of ethics in contrast with Hebrew limitations, not only a deepening of moral understanding and obligation, but it was supremely his personal embodiment of the ethical ideal.[4]

"But put ye on the Lord Jesus Christ, and make not provision for the flesh, to fulfill the lusts thereof" (Romans 13:14).

EIGHT

THE HOPE OF THE WORLD

JOHN F. WALVOORD

Dr. Walvoord is generally recognized as one of the leading conservative evangelical theologians of America. He was educated at Wheaton College (A.B.), Texas Christian University (A.M.), and Dallas Theological Seminary (Th.B., Th.M., Th.D.). He has been a member of the faculty of Dallas Theological Seminary since 1936 as Professor of Systematic Theology and Registrar, and as President since 1952. He is Editor of Bibliotheca Sacra, *and is the author of works on* The Holy Spirit (1943), The Return of the Lord (1955), The Thessalonian Epistles (1955), The Rapture Question (1957), *and* The Millennial Kingdom (1959).

Modern man is like a jet pilot flying on instruments. He is conscious of the tremendous speed of life. He has a measure of confidence in his heritage, in his scientific achievements, and in the instruments that are at his disposal. He thinks that he can foresee the immediate future; but beyond that there is fog and uncertainty and the gnawing fear that some obstacle, not indicated by his instruments or seen too late, may smash into nothing his fragile ship.

Modern thought, whether stated in the intricate metaphysics of the philosopher or in the undeveloped thinking of the ordinary man, tends to question the certainty of hope. Religious hope is often discounted as mythical or emotional. Its alternatives also are viewed with suspicion. The theory of organic evolution confidently advanced by a previous generation as the hope of the scientific and philosophic world does not seem to have practical relevance to the present world. The whole idea of progress is suspect, and there is apprehension that perhaps things are going to be worse rather than better.

Confidence in the ability of man to solve his problems likewise has been shaken by the events of the first half of the twentieth century. Civilization certainly has not achieved world peace or security for the individual. Culture does not seem to have solved the moral and intellectual problems of life. The scientific achievements which have demonstrated the ingenuity of man seem only to complicate the problem with great weapons of destruction and more causes for despair. Even in the field of physical causation, an element of indeterminism has been introduced by the discovery that atomic motion cannot be precisely predicted. Based on such elements as are observable in the world, there is little ground for hope, and there is also the fear of the unknown that stretches beyond physical death.

Though an air of skepticism and pessimism characterizes our day, most men have not carried it to its logical conclusion, and have tended to erase the disquiet which possesses the soul by the fevered activity of labor toward human goals. Pleasure, diversion, and entertainment are the order of the day. Even religion is sometimes an escape rather than a true ground for hope, and too often is a blind

worship of an unknown god instead of an intelligent Christian faith.

In spite of prevalent unbelief in the reality of hope, the human heart inevitably longs for a better tomorrow. As the growing flower lifts its petals to the sun, so human expectation directs its attention to the future. Every politician promises that tomorrow will not be as yesterday. Every scientist dreams of further conquests of the physical world. Every astronomer anticipates discovering another star. Even the communist world holds before its captives the lure of the utopia that will come with a classless society. Hope springs eternal in the human breast. As Emil Brunner states in introducing his book *Eternal Hope*, "What oxygen is for the lungs, such is hope for the meaning of human life. Take oxygen away and death occurs through suffocation, take hope away and humanity is constricted through lack of breath; despair supervenes, spelling the paralysis of intellectual and spiritual powers by a feeling of the senselessness and purposelessness of existence." [1]

Modern man, however, is short of breath. Though he cannot live without hope, he has not been satisfied by the future that extends before him. Never has there been more insecurity, uncertainty, or fear than that which grips the modern mind. Only the anesthetic of indifference, carelessness, and occupation with the present has made the hopelessness of modern man endurable. It is in such a dark context that the eternal hope which is in Christ shines like a shaft of brilliant sunlight in a background of clouds. The warm assuring rays of revelation which come from God and of hope which spring from a source far beyond the storms of life have brought the restless minds of countless souls to certainty and calm assurance. The experience embodied in

the hymn by William H. Burleigh is the experience of the
one who has found life in Christ.

> Our eyes see dimly till by faith anointed,
> And our blind choosing brings us grief and pain;
> Through Him alone Who hath our way appointed,
> We find our peace again.[2]

Christian hope is completely and totally Biblical. Though
confirmed by experience and supported rationally by the
theologian, it depends upon the authority of Scripture.
Modern unbelief and disillusionment have their roots in
departure from the Scriptures and in denial of their inspiration and infallibility. Only hope that is grounded in Scripture
is legitimate. Beyond a limited projection of his experience,
man has no power to delineate any sure hope of the future.
Though many non-Christian religions have interested men,
as witnessed by the millions of their adherents, the hope
that is therein contained is without ground, and is a
superstitious surmise with no authority beyond the wishful
thinking of those who embrace it. Most of the religious
writings of the world apart from the Bible do not attempt
an ordered eschatology. Their concept of the future state
is either vague and incomplete, or, like Islam, is derived
from supposed revelations which borrowed in part from
the Bible.

The Holy Scriptures present the only comprehensive
eschatology which has ever been offered to man in written
form. Its doctrine of future things is not incidental or
occasional, but is a dominant theme in some of its principal
books and is inevitably included in almost any presentation
of Biblical revelation. Over half of the eschatology of
Scripture has already been realized, and countless prophecies

of men and nations once given by divine inspiration of God have in the course of human events had their literal fulfillment. It is therefore most reasonable to project those prophecies yet unfulfilled as a part of the certain purpose of God and to believe that just as fulfilled prophecy has demonstrated the accuracy and infallibility of the prophetic Word, so the future also as it unfolds will not let one word of Scripture fall to the ground. The Christian hope is a Scriptural hope, and the Christian rests not in the words of philosophies of men, but in the certainty and validity of the Word of God.

Christian hope is not offered in the Scriptures as an option which man is free to choose, but as the only way of life provided by God for time or eternity. It is unique and indispensable, realized through the person and work of Christ. Christian hope is simply and completely faith in Christ. The Apostle Peter stated it positively and succinctly as he stood before the threatening Sanhedrin: "Neither is there salvation in any other: for there is none other name under heaven given among men, whereby we must be saved" (Acts 4:12). The Apostle Paul states the same truth when he refers to those who "were without Christ" as "strangers from the covenants of promise, having no hope, and without God in the world" (Eph. 2:12).

The same finality is contained in the very terms of the gospel: "He that believeth on Him is not condemned: but he that believeth not is condemned already, because he hath not believed in the name of the only begotten Son of God" (John 3:18). Again in similar words: "He that believeth on the Son hath everlasting life: and he that believeth not the Son shall not see life; but the wrath of God abideth on him" (John 3:36). From Genesis to Revelation Jesus Christ is presented as the indispensable and only Saviour. There is no true Christian hope apart from Him; in fact, there is no hope at all except as it depends on the Son of God.

Countless Scriptures present the unique and incomparable person of Christ and the completeness and accuracy of His finished work in His death and resurrection. The Saviour of men is none other than God Himself who in becoming the Saviour became man, and who in accomplishing His work died on the cross of Calvary as the supreme sacrifice for sin. Just as Christ is the only person to whom one may go for salvation, so the work of Christ is the only ground for forgiveness, cleansing, and justification. The unique quality of hope grounded in Christ at once distinguishes the true evangelical faith from all its counterfeits.

Christian hope does not rest upon mere attitudes of worship, emotional or aesthetic experiences, or upon the moral and ethical works of men. Until an individual soul comes to that point of decision where Jesus Christ is recognized as the Son of God, as the object of worship, faith, and obedience, until by the grace of God he receives Jesus Christ as his personal Saviour, there is no legitimate ground for hope. Like the Ephesian Christians he is labeled by Scripture as "dead in trespasses and sins" (Eph. 2:1). But when saved by grace through faith (Eph. 2:8), whether Jew or Gentile, he is reconciled unto God (Eph. 2:16). The essential and integral absolutes of Christian faith declare that hope that is not Christian, hope that is not fixed in Christ, is not hope at all.

Though "the substance of things hoped for, the evidence of things not seen" is faith (Heb. 11:1), it is faith that is supported by solid facts of history. A Christian can be confident of the future because of historic certainties in the past. The structure of Christian hope is based upon a foundation which is fully adequate to support it. Modern liberalism which rejects the prophetic future usually rejects Biblical history as well. The contents of the Holy Scriptures were obviously not delivered first to the present generation, but were written by the Holy Spirit as a contemporary message. They were a record of divine dealing with men, and constituted an exhortation to immediate action even if presented in a context of hope for the future. The Scriptures not only reveal the God of the universe in all His infinite majesty and perfection of His attributes, but they reveal God in action, God dealing with human beings and human situations.

The God of Scripture is revealed as a God of purpose, a God of sovereignty, a God who has not disclosed everything, but a God who has provided the materials and substance for a faith that is intelligent. The Scriptures, therefore, record what God has done in the past as He has dealt with sin and human failure. The Scriptures affirm the promises of God, the certainty of their fulfillment, whether predictions of grace or judgment. The Scriptures reveal the providence of God in His sovereignty, even in a world that is confused, sinful, and rebellious. The Scriptures reveal a purpose moving through the pages of human history. There is no true philosophy of human history except as it is given in Scripture, and the many attempts of men to give meaning to history apart from Scripture are their own refutation.

It is clear from Scripture that God's central purpose is to reveal Himself, His infinite perfections, His sovereign grace, His love, and His righteousness, faithfulness and goodness. The universe as a whole, as well as human history in its detail, ultimately has its meaning as pointing us to the God who created the world and who has brought its history into being. As a major factor of the divine purpose, the Scriptures reveal God's desire and willingness to save from judgment those who turn to Him. The coats of skin provided Adam and Eve in their nakedness, the bloody altar of Abel, the triumphant faith of Abraham, the intricate system of sacrifice in the Mosaic Law, as well as the supreme sacrifice of Christ on the cross, all point to the salvation of sinners as one of God's central purposes.

The ways and purposes of God, however, are infinitely complex. The Scriptures reveal that God has a place and a purpose for each individual and for each nation, and that in particular He has a place for Israel in the past, present, and future. In the present age He is fulfilling His purpose to call out a people for His name from all nations, Jew and Gentile alike. His purposes include the consummation promised in the prophetic Word. Students of Scripture, while reveling in the completeness of divine revelation, nevertheless must confess that they know only a fragment of the whole. With Paul they must exclaim: "O the depth of the riches both of the wisdom and knowledge of God! How unsearchable are his judgments, and his ways past finding out! For who hath known the mind of the Lord? or who hath been his counsellor?" (Rom. 11:33-34).

Christian hope, therefore, is not an isolated future that is detached from the past, but from our point of view in time is that part of the purpose of God which is yet unfulfilled. When the future has unfolded, it undoubtedly will reveal the same God we know now, the same providential and sovereign attributes, and same completeness of grace, wisdom, and righteousness. Hope, as it is in Christ, is therefore not vain, nor is it wishful thinking, nor the idealistic speculations of the optimist who hopes for the best with no ground for his hope. It is that solid promise given in the Word of God, that just as God has been faithful in the past, so He will also be in the future.

Christian hope as it is presented in the Scripture was never intended to be a distant expectation with no relevance to the present scene. In fact, the greatest prophecies of Scripture as embodied in the major prophetic books of the Old Testament, as well as the prophetic contribution of the New Testament, were framed by the exigencies of the time, the desperate need of people for light, courage, and exhortation. Some of the grandest themes of prophecy were delivered in the darkest hours when sin and apostasy seemed to be engulfing the people of God and erasing all possibility of future grace and mercy. Prophecy as it is contained in the Scriptures was ever intended to be a commentary on the present as well as to give intelligent direction for the future.

L. S. Chafer has said: "Knowledge of Biblical prophecy qualifies all Christian life and service." [3] Not only does prophecy demonstrate God's faithfulness in keeping His Word, but it gives to the believer a sense of direction, purpose, and meaning to life. The present is interpreted in the light of the future. The sorrows and trials of the present are alleviated by the certain hope of deliverance that is coming. The moral decisions of life are given meaning by their ultimate value in eternity. The Christian hope purifies the heart, clarifies the vision, strengthens the weary hand, and sheds the glory of the future upon the present.

The familiar allegation that the study of prophecy is impractical and irrelevant, that we should seek to live in one world at a time, that we should avoid the starry futurism which supposedly causes us to stumble at the present, is unjustified from any point of view. Biblical prophecy and the Christian hope, properly understood, are the divine light of the future shed upon the present. It was not the divine intention that anyone should be so occupied with future things as to neglect his present opportunity, to minimize his personal responsibility, or fail to live each moment to the full. Prophecy was intended instead to give the ultimate meaning to the contemporary situation.

Just as the historic ground of Christian faith has its ultimate resting place upon the person and work of Christ in His first coming, so the eschatological hope which is yet future depends upon the return of Christ. The certainty and detail of the Christian hope are in direct proportion to the certainty and literal character of the second coming of our Lord and Saviour Jesus Christ. This has been recognized from the early centuries of the Christian church. The early church fathers saw that the only hope of the world was inseparably linked to the future coming of the Lord Jesus Christ.

The longing for perfect government, righteousness, equity, economic prosperity, deliverance from the insecurity and fears which plague the modern world, finds its answer in the prospect of the return of Christ and the establishment of His kingdom. The Scriptures reveal no other solution for the problems of the world than the return of Christ with its accompanying purging judgments and divine intervention in human affairs. The doctrine of the premillennial return of Christ is both a profound philosophy of history and a comprehensive theological answer to questions which have been raised concerning the sovereignty, goodness, and wisdom of God as challenged by human sin, depravity, and misery.

The return of Christ is likewise the event upon which hangs the expectation of Israel for fulfillment of her covenant promises. To Abraham God gave the extensive promises that He would make of his seed a great nation, that He would bless those who blessed Israel and curse those who cursed Abraham's seed. Through Abraham was to come the promised seed, Christ, who would be a blessing to all nations. In addition to these general blessings to Abraham and his seed was the promise of possession of the land from the River of Egypt to the River Euphrates (Gen. 15:18). This promise of the land as an everlasting possession of Israel (Gen. 17:8) obviously required the continuance of the nation forever as assured by the later prophets (Jer. 31:35-37).

These promises were given extensive confirmation in the many Old Testament references to the possession of the land in the coming kingdom age. The major and minor prophets of the Old Testament reiterate in hundreds of verses the theme that Israel though chastened, disciplined, and scattered by divine judgments would nevertheless be regathered from the ends of the earth and restored to its ancient land. Further confirmation of the hope of Israel was given in the promise to David that God would continue his royal house and line forever, the literal fulfillment of which requires the return of Christ and His rule over His ancient people restored and regathered in their Promised Land.

The general truth of the return of the Lord is supremely the hope of the church, and constitutes the climax and consummation of the divine program as it relates to the present age. Many expositors distinguish the return of Christ for His church from the return of Christ to establish His earthly kingdom. Both of these eschatological events are inseparably related to the fulfillment of God's promises to the saints in the present age. The Christian hope, however, is directed particularly to spiritual and eternal things rather than to the millennial earth and the fulfillment of the kingdom promises. The content of this hope includes expectation of bodily resurrection or the translation and transformation of living saints, the hope of complete sanctification, that is, personal holiness suited for the immediate presence of a holy God, hope of reward and recognition of service for God, hope of eternal fellowship in the heavenly Jerusalem in the new heavens and the new earth. These items of faith are peculiarly the expectation of those who have put their trust in Christ.

The truth of bodily resurrection in its widest sense belongs to all men. The Scriptures constantly hold before the saints the prospect of a resurrection body. Even Job who lived before the day of written Scripture seemed to understand this expectation (Job 19:25-26). The New Testament is especially complete in its presentation of this truth. Even those who are not classified as saints are assured of their ultimate resurrection and divine judgment (Rev. 20:11-15). The fact of this resurrection was emphasized by Christ Himself when He declared: "The hour is coming, in the which all that are in the graves shall hear his voice, and shall come forth; they that have done good, unto the resurrection of life; and they that have done evil, unto the resurrection of damnation" (John 5:28-29). The Old Testament doctrine is equally explicit. In Daniel 12:2 it is prophesied: "And many of them that sleep in the dust of the earth shall awake, some to everlasting life, and some to shame and everlasting contempt." As a practical hope and joyous expectation, however, it is embraced only by the saints.

The doctrine of the resurrection of saints is given comprehensive treatment in I Corinthians 15. The great truth is presented that Christ Himself rose from the dead, and became the ground for the hope of the resurrection of all men. In the exposition of the doctrine of resurrection it is made clear first of all that apart from the resurrection of Christ there would be no assurance of the resurrection of all men (I Cor. 15:12–19). It is further established that not all will be raised at the same time. Christ was raised three days after His death and became the token, or firstfruits, of the future resurrection (I Cor. 15:20). The resurrection of the saints is specifically related in I Corinthians 15:23 to the coming of Christ. "But every man in his own order: Christ the firstfruits; afterward they that are Christ's at his coming." It is intimated that the final resurrection is a later event in connection with the end (I Cor. 15:24). This is made more explicit in Revelation 20, where the millennium, or thousand-year reign of Christ, separates the first resurrection from the final resurrection in connection with the great white throne judgment.

Considerable attention is given in I Corinthians 15 to the necessity of resurrection. Human bodies as now possessed by men in the flesh are weak, subject to age and decay, and are doomed to physical death. They are therefore not suited for use throughout eternity and must be replaced. The normal order is that of death and resurrection. The nature of the resurrection body is defined in I Corinthians 15 as a "spiritual body" (I Cor. 15:44). It is further defined as having "the image of the heavenly" and as possessing incorruption and immortality (I Cor. 15:48–49, 53). The resurrection body of the saints must not be confused with the characteristics of those who have on occasion been restored from the grave as, for instance, in the case of Lazarus. The type and pattern of the resurrection body of a believer are those of the body of Christ Himself.

From the postresurrection ministry of Christ certain important facts can be established. Christ states of His resurrection body that it possesses flesh and bones (Luke 24:39). It is apparent that He could eat (Luke 24:41–43), but it is never said of Christ after His resurrection that He was hungry or thirsty, nor is it stated in Scripture that He slept. From the incident of Christ talking with His disciples on the road to Emmaus (Luke 24:31–35), it is evident that the resurrection body of Christ could be seen and that under normal circumstances it could be recognized (cf. John 20:11–16). It seems evident, however, that the resurrection body of Christ was not subject to all the limitations of our present natural bodies. Though He could walk, He did not necessarily avail Himself of ordinary means of human transportation, as indicated by the fact that He appeared to the ten disciples in Jerusalem (Luke 24:36) when He had last appeared at Emmaus. Again it is recorded that He was able to come into a room when the doors had been shut without being hindered physically by the barriers (John 20:19). It is also significant that His resurrection body bore the marks of His crucifixion (John 20:20).

Some of these characteristics of the resurrection body of Christ may be unique. It is evident that the usual glory which attends the person of Christ was veiled during His resurrection ministry and was not released until after His ascension. Possibly the believer's body in heaven will share some of the glory which is characteristic of the heavenly sphere. It may not be true for the saints ordinarily that they will bear the marks of conflict in this present world as Christ retained His wounds: presumably handicaps and shortcomings of physical bodies in this life will be replaced by perfection in eternity, those who die in infancy undoubtedly will be mature, and those who have suffered disability will have the normal functions of a resurrection body. The hope of bodily resurrection is a sure and important aspect of the Christian faith, and is generally integral to the creeds of all who accept the inspiration of Scripture.

Students of eschatology have not all agreed as to the

time and order of resurrection. Amillenarians view the future as holding one general resurrection in which all, both righteous and unrighteous, will be raised and finally judged before entrance into the eternal state. Premillenarians usually distinguish the resurrection of the saints before the millennial reign of Christ from the final resurrection before the judgment of the great white throne in Revelation 20, and thereby establish a chronology of a minimum of three major resurrections; namely, the resurrection of Christ already fulfilled, the resurrection of the saints in connection with the second coming of Christ before the millennium, and the resurrection of the wicked after the millennium. Some make further divisions by establishing the resurrection of the church, or of believers of this present age, as occurring before the time of tribulation predicted as preceding the return of the Lord. These are generally described by the term *pretribulationist* in contrast to the *posttribulationists* who view the saints of all ages as being raised at the same time in connection with the return of Christ. These differences of interpretation of Scripture, dependent somewhat upon prophetic interpretation relating to a future millennial kingdom and the eschatology of Israel, should not be construed as in any sense making uncertain the central fact of bodily resurrection for all the saints. It should be clear to any student of Scripture that the hope of bodily resurrection is integral to the Christian faith, as is made clear in the First Epistle of Paul to the Corinthians: "If in this life only we have hope in Christ, we are of all men most miserable" (I Cor. 15:19).

The theme of the translation of the saints at the return of the Lord is one of the distinctive doctrines of the New Testament. Though the Old Testament refers repeatedly to the return of the Lord and the resurrection of the dead, nowhere does the Old Testament revelation speak of the translation of all the saints at the coming of the Lord. In fact, the universal representation of the Old Testament pictures the saints who are on the earth at the time of the return of the Lord as remaining in the earthly sphere, in their natural bodies, and therein entering the millennial kingdom. This constitutes one of the important reasons why some expositors believe that the translation of the church is an earlier event separated by some years from the return of the Lord to the earth.

The content of the revelation concerning translation is given in two principal New Testament passages, I Corinthians 15:51–52 and I Thessalonians 4:13–18. According to the Corinthians passage, the truth of the rapture of the church is a mystery, that is, a truth revealed in the New Testament which was hidden from Old Testament revelation. Paul wrote the Corinthians: "Behold, I shew you a mystery; We shall not all sleep, but we shall all be changed, in a moment, in the twinkling of an eye, at the last trump: for the trumpet shall sound, and the dead shall be raised incorruptible, and we shall be changed" (I Cor. 15:51–52). That not all saints would die before the coming of the Lord is not the precise point of this divine revelation. It is rather that without dying they would all be changed, or translated, from natural, mortal bodies to spiritual, immortal bodies. This was to be accomplished, not by the normal route of death and resurrection, but "in a moment, in the twinkling of an eye, at the last trump." This trump is identified by most expositors with that mentioned in I Thessalonians 4:16.

The question had arisen in the Thessalonian church concerning the order of events between the translation of the church, which they had been taught, and the resurrection of the dead in Christ. The question had apparently been raised whether the dead in Christ would be raised at a later time, possibly in connection with the establishment of the millennial kingdom rather than the coming of Christ for His church. In answer to this Paul writes the Thessalonians: "For the Lord himself shall descend from heaven with a shout, with the voice of the archangel, and with the trump of God: and the dead in Christ shall rise first: then we which are alive and remain shall be caught up together with them in the clouds, to meet the Lord in the air: and so shall we ever be with the Lord" (I Thess. 4:16, 17). The Thessalonian question is therefore answered by the revelation that the resurrection of the dead in Christ will occur a moment before the translation of the living saints. The Thessalonians are therefore comforted and encouraged, not only in the hope of the coming of the Lord to relieve them from their time of trial and trouble by translation from this world, but also with the prospect that on that occasion they would see their loved ones in Christ again, and that the fellowship thus realized would never be terminated.

Scholarly debate has continued to the present on some of the details of this prophecy. Posttribulationists have pointed to the fact that the resurrection of the dead and the translation of the living occur at approximately the same time, and, inasmuch as the resurrection is commonly associated with the return of Christ to establish His millennial kingdom after the predicted time of tribulation, this would be conclusive proof of the posttribulational position. Pretribulationists have replied, however, by noting that the expression "dead in Christ" is a particular phrase and that the theological import of the clause "in Christ" is consistently used in the New Testament to refer to saints of the church in this present age, and is never used of Old Testament saints. Hence, they have found confirmation in this passage of the pretribulation position. They have noted also the fact that the coming of the Lord is to be a doctrine of comfort which is seemingly incongruous with the thought of the church going through the awful time of trial and trouble of which Christ Himself spoke (Matt. 24:15–22) and which many identify with fulfillment of the last seven years of Daniel's prophecy concerning Israel (Dan. 9:24–27).

In contrast to prophecies that speak of the return of Christ to establish His earthly kingdom, the fulfillment of which is preceded by a definite sequence of signs (Matt. 24:15–30), the translation of the church, or "the rapture" as it is often called (from *rapio*, Latin Vulgate for "caught up"; I Thess. 4:17), is uniformly presented as an immediate prospect of the church and an item for daily expectation. The early church fathers, puzzled by the seeming contradiction of a daily expectation of the Lord's coming and the predicted tribulation which is said to precede, solved the problem in some instances at least by assuming that the trials they were then experiencing were the time of the tribulation, in contradiction of Paul's instruction to the Thessalonians in 2 Thessalonians 2:1–12 where he corrected a similar teaching in the Thessalonian church. Nothing is plainer than that the early church never dreamed that the coming of Christ was postponed by a thousand years more or less, nor is there any clear teaching in the first two centuries of the church that the interadvent age was the millennium. Christians of the first and immediately succeeding centuries seem to have believed that Christ could have come at any time, and that the prophecies relating to His coming would have their literal fulfillment.

The hope of the translation of the church has never been more justified than in the twentieth century. Whatever difficulties there may have been in relation to events which seemingly had to occur first, such as the death of Peter, a long life for Paul, the destruction of Jerusalem, and similar prophecies, none of these obstacles now stand in the way. Millions of evangelical Christians in time of sorrow, affliction, and testing have been comforted by this blessed hope that Jesus is coming, and that without announcement or warning they might, in the twinkling of an eye, find themselves in the presence of the Lord to be with Him forever. This is the Christian hope. One of the tragedies of contemporary theology is that in moving away from faith in the authority and inspiration of Scripture they have lost also this precious hope of the Lord's return.

The longing of the human breast for a true holiness and conformity to the will of God is to be satisfied completely when believers in Christ see Him face to face. This is the faithful promise of many Scriptures. The Apostle John wrote in his first epistle: "Beloved, now are we the sons of God, and it doth not yet appear what we shall be: but we know that, when he shall appear, we shall be like him; for we shall see him as he is" (I John 3:2). Paul in writing the Ephesian church concerning the ultimate sanctification of the believer pictures the bride of Christ in these words: "A glorious church, not having spot, or wrinkle, or any such thing; but that it should be holy and without blemish" (Eph. 5:27). Paul also wrote the Philippians concerning the transformation of the human body: "For our conversation is in heaven; from whence also we look for the Saviour, the Lord Jesus Christ: who shall change our vile body, that it may be fashioned like unto his glorious body, according to the working whereby he is able even to subdue all things unto himself" (Phil. 3:20–21). Similar expressions elsewhere in Scripture assure the believer in Christ that whatever struggles with temptations and whatever frustrations of

moral limitation may be experienced in this life, once the
believer meets Christ face to face these imperfections will
flee. The transformed and sanctified saint in glory will be
an exhibit of what the grace of God can do (Eph. 2:7).
Though claims to complete holiness in this life seem to be
an illusion, it will then be the possession of everyone who
has put his trust in Christ. Throughout eternity to come
there will not be one sin to trouble the soul, one stain of
impurity to embarrass the believer in the presence of a holy
God.

The normal course for all men according to Hebrews 9:27
is that "it is appointed unto men once to die, but after this
the judgment." Both those who meet God through death
and resurrection and those saints who are translated without
seeing death are the subject of a divine judgment that has
to do with their reward for service. Future judgments are
related primarily to works, in the case of those who are
not saved as well as for the saint. Though salvation is by
grace and is a gift of God, there is divine recognition of
difference in service. Reference to this judgment is found in
II Corinthians 5:10 where Paul wrote: "For we must all
appear before the judgment seat of Christ; that every one
may receive the things done in his body, according to that
he hath done, whether it be good or bad." It has to do
therefore not with the question of eternal destiny, but with
the evaluation of works. According to his earlier letter in
I Corinthians, the purpose of this judgment is not punishment but reward for service. Paul uses the figure of a building built upon a supplied foundation. He identifies works as
comparable to six materials used in the building: gold,
silver, precious stones, wood, hay, stubble (I Cor. 3:12).
He declares further: "Every man's work shall be made
manifest: for the day shall declare it, because it shall be

revealed by fire; and the fire shall try every man's work of what sort it is" (v. 13). It is obvious that fire would consume wood, hay, and stubble, whereas gold, silver, and precious stones are by their nature incombustible. They abide when wood, hay, and stubble are destroyed. The application of this figure is made in verse 14. "If any man's work abide which he hath built thereupon, he shall receive a reward. If any man's work shall be burned, he shall suffer loss: but he himself shall be saved; yet so as by fire" (vv. 14–15). That which survives the fire is the basis for reward. That which is consumed is lost, but in no case does it result in the loss of salvation, for salvation is by grace and not by works: "He himself shall be saved; yet so as by fire." In that day every account will be settled; every sacrifice made and every burden borne will be evaluated by the omniscient God whose faithfulness and righteousness will allow no good work to fall to the ground unrewarded.

The interpretation of prophecies indicating a future reign of Christ on the earth for one thousand years is a major area of disagreement in Biblical theology. Probably the most popular approach in contemporary theology may be described as amillennial, that is, a denial of the teaching that a thousand-year reign will follow the return of Christ. Amillennialism is of course the position of liberal as well as of neo-orthodox scholars. The Roman Catholic Church has been almost entirely amillennial since the days of Augustine. Strict followers of Calvin and Luther in the ranks of conservatives are likewise amillennial. It is generally conceded, however, that the majority view of the early church for at least two or three centuries was chiliastic or premillennial. The most prevalent amillennial interpretation that the reign of Christ began with His first advent and terminates with His second advent does not seem to have occurred to any of the early fathers, even though some of them were somewhat confused in their eschatology.

The idea that the thousand-year reign of Christ is yet future, but that it will constitute the last thousand years of the interadvent period, a view known as postmillennialism, is a comparatively modern idea and is usually traced by its adherents to Daniel Whitby, a seventeenth-century Unitarian controversialist. Though this view was the major contender against amillennialism in conservative theology in the last half of the nineteenth century it has been practically abandoned by most scholars.

The major opponent of amillennialism today is premillennialism, that view which anticipates the second advent of Christ as preceding and inaugurating a thousand-year reign of Christ upon the earth. Except for some sects which are erratic in their eschatology, premillenarians are usually conservative in their general theology, and normally are to be found only among adherents to the doctrine of Scriptural infallibility. The two essentials of premillennialism are the complete authority and accuracy of Scripture and the literal interpretation of promises relative to an earthly reign of Christ.

The Scriptures present the doctrine of the millennium as a major theme of revelation. Chapter after chapter of the Old Testament voices the prophetic utterance of a future period in history when Israel will be regathered from its scattered condition, restored, honored, and blessed, and will possess the land promised to Abraham. The king of Israel is described as the Immanuel who will reign upon the throne of David (Isa. 7:14; 9:6–7). His government will be one of perfect righteousness (Isa. 11) and, although His reign will be absolute, there will be universal joy, peace, and economic prosperity in the earth. Literal fulfillment of these prophecies is impossible in the present world, and premillenarians therefore hold to future fulfillment.

The length of the reign of Christ is specified as a thousand years in Revelation 20 with important events occurring before the thousand years and others after the thousand years, thereby indicating a literal period of time. The millennium is a time not only of Israel's blessing, but one in which all nations will share the beneficent reign of Christ. Though it has an obvious governmental character, its main features are spiritual realities such as joy, peace, holiness, and righteousness. The resurrected saints of all classifications are apparently associated with Christ in His reign over the earth, but probably resident in the heavenly city, the new Jerusalem, even though they may participate to some extent in earthly events. The picture provided in Scripture does not supply all details, but nevertheless establishes the principal characteristics of the millennial period. According to Revelation 20, the millennium will end with the loosing of Satan who had been bound at its beginning, and with the rebellion of some of those who had been born during the millennium. They are consumed by a judgment of fire and the devil himself is cast into the lake of fire and brimstone (Rev. 20:7–10). The conclusion of the millennium is followed by the judgment of the great white throne, apparently a judgment of wicked dead who are raised at that time. A new heaven and a new earth are created as the scene for the eternal state.

Considering the extensive revelation concerning the millennial kingdom, it is perhaps strange that there is such limited revelation concerning the eternal state which will follow. This is probably dictated, however, by the fact that there is no real necessity of our knowing the details of our eternal state beyond a general description which will assure us of a future of blessedness, joy, and peace. The picture of

the new heaven and the new earth is given principally in
Revelation, chapter 21. The opening eight verses describe
the scene as one in which there is no more death, sorrow, or
crying and where former things have passed away (Rev.
21:4). Excluded from the new heaven and the new earth are
all the wicked who have their part in the lake of fire (Rev.
21:8). Most of the twenty-first chapter of Revelation is
devoted to a description of new Jerusalem, the heavenly city
which apparently was in existence during the millennial reign
of Christ, but not on the earth. With the creation of the new
heaven and the new earth, however, the "great city, the holy
Jerusalem" (Rev. 21:10), descends to the earth and rests
there throughout eternity.

Expositors differ as to the extent in which the description
of the new Jerusalem should be taken literally. The city
described as measuring 1500 miles in length, breadth, and
height is variously conceived as a cube or pyramid, lighted
by the glory of God and constituting the residence of the
saints of all ages. The eternal bliss of residence in this
heavenly city is the ultimate Christian hope and the terminus
of all prophecies relating to the blessed.

The Apostle Peter contemplating the destruction of the
present earth and the creation of the new heavens and the
new earth made this practical application: "Seeing then that
all these things shall be dissolved, what manner of persons
ought ye to be in all holy conversation and godliness, looking for and hasting unto the coming of the day of God,
wherein the heavens being on fire shall be dissolved, and
the elements shall melt with fervent heat? Nevertheless we,
according to his promise, look for new heavens and a new
earth, wherein dwelleth righteousness. Wherefore, beloved,
seeing that ye look for such things, be diligent that ye be
found of him in peace, without spot, and blameless" (II Pet.

3:11–14). The prophetic hope of the world was never intended by God to be an area of theological debate, but rather a magnetic goal, attracting the pilgrim saint as he struggles, stumbles, and yet climbs upward. The dawn of the coming eternal day, with its hope for the world and especially for the saint, casts its glow upon the present path and gives perspective and meaning to every human situation.

NOTES

I. MAN'S DILEMMA: SIN

1. "The Lost Dimension of Religion," *The Saturday Evening Post*, June 14, 1958.

II. THE AUTHORITY OF THE BIBLE

1. William Temple, "Revelation" (John Baillie and Hugh Martin, *Revelation*, ed.) (New York: Macmillan, 1927), p. 83.

2. Material for this paragraph as well as for certain other parts of this essay originally formed part of the Griffith-Thomas Lectures printed in *Bibliotheca Sacra*, April 1958 to January 1959. Permission to use this material was given by the editor.

3. *Modern Man in Search of a Soul* (New York: Harcourt, Brace & Co., 1935), pp. 264ff.

4. *Faith and Reason* (New York: Harper & Bros., 1946), pp. ix and x.

5. It is no accident that all three great periods of speculative philosophy, ancient, medieval, and modern, though beginning with brave asseverations as to the meaning of existence, have fizzled out on a dismal note of skepticism.

6. "Letter to Jerome," *The Confessions and Letters of St. Augustine* ("A Select Library of the Nicene and Post-Nicene Fathers of the Christian Church," Vol. I, LXXXII, Sec. 3; Buffalo: The Christian Literature Company, 1886–89), p. 350.

7. L. Gaussen, *The Inspiration of the Holy Scriptures* (Chicago: Moody Press, 1940), pp. 139–40.

8. "Vom Missbrauch der Messe" in *Dr. Martin Luthers polemische deutsche Schriften*, ed. Johann Konrad Armischer (Erlangen: Carl Heyder, 1833), xxviii, p. 35.

9. *Institutes of the Christian Religion*, trans. Henry Beveridge (Edinburgh: Calvin Translation Society, 1845), III, 166; II, 402;

Commentaries on the Epistle of Paul to the Hebrews, trans. John Owen (Edinburgh: Calvin Translation Society, 1855), p. xxi.

10. For the Lutheran position, see the Augsburg Confession, Article XXVIII; for the Calvinistic, see the Canons of the Synod of Dort, Articles IV and V, and the Westminster Confession, Article XIV:2; for the Anglican, see the Thirty-nine Articles, Section XX; and for the Baptist (Northern Churches), see the New Hampshire Confession, Article I. All of these are available in Philip Schaff, *Creeds of Christendom* (New York: Harper & Bros., 1919), Vol. III.

11. *Story of the Bible* (London: Vision Press, Ltd., 1952), p. 277.

12. *An Outline of Biblical Theology* (Philadelphia: Westminster Press, 1946), pp. 9, 44.

13. *The Theology of Crisis* (New York: Charles Scribner's Sons, 1929), p. 9.

14. "The Author's Preface to the English Translation," *The Epistle to the Romans* (London: Oxford University Press, 1933), p. v.

15. *The Word of God and the Word of Man*, trans. Douglas Hort (Grand Rapids, Mich.: Zondervan, 1935), pp. 44, 50.

16. *The Mediator* (New York: Macmillan, 1942), p. 185.

17. *The Theology of Crisis*, p. 41. Cf. also *Christian Doctrine of God* (London: Lutterworth, 1949), p. 12.

18. *Das Christliche Verständnis der Offenbarung* (München: Chr. Kaiser, 1948), p. 29.

19. Pp. 3, 34. See also Karl Barth, *Kirchliche Dogmatik* (4 vols. Zurich: Evangelischer Verlag, 1932), Vol. III, Part I, p. 25.

20. "*Kalupto*," *Theologisches Wörterbuch* (Stuttgart: Von W. Kahlhammer, 1938), *in loco*.

21. *Revelation and Reason* (Philadelphia: Westminster, 1946), p. 8.

22. *Kirchliche Dogmatik*, I, 2, p. 587.

23. Ibid. p. 587.

24. Ibid. p. 594.

25. See Reinhold Niebuhr, *Beyond Tragedy: Essays on the*

Christian Interpretation of History (New York: Charles Scrib-
ner's Sons, 1937), p. 23; and Hans Werner Bartsch (ed.),
Kerygma and Myth: A Theological Debate, trans. Reginald H.
Fuller (London: S.P.C.K., 1953).

26. Paul Jewett documents this same criticism of Emil Brunner in his monograph *Emil Brunner's Doctrine of Scripture*
(London: J. Clarke, 1954), pp. 168–72.

27. *Kirchliche Dogmatik,* Vol. I, Part II, pp. 592, 595.

28. See also Galatians 1:16, "to reveal his son." The final condemnation of the heathen is not that they are ignorant but that
they are unthankful and do not worship God (Romans 1:18ff.).

29. Biblically this may be stated in the following manner.
With respect to Jesus Christ as redeemer, "There is none other
name under heaven given among men whereby ye must be
saved" (Acts 4:12). "But now once in the end of the world
hath he appeared to put away sin by the sacrifice of himself"
(Hebrews 9:26). The role of prophet, however, Jesus Christ
shared with others. "A prophet shall the Lord your God raise
up unto you of your brethren like unto me . . . his Son Jesus"
(Acts 3:22 and 26). Though He was not the only one to act as
prophet, He was a unique prophet, for He not only revealed God
in a unique way ("Never man spake like this man," John 7:46);
He, unlike all other prophets, *is* the revealed One ("He who hath
builded the house hath more honor than the house," Hebrews
3:1–6).

30. *The Philosophy of Revelation* (3rd ed.; New York: Harper & Bros. 1940), p. 256.

31. Of the New Testament examples which he specifically
cites as in one class or the other, Bauer lists six usages of
apokalupto as referring to revelation of ideas as true and nine
instances in which the object is a person. With the noun form,
apokalupsis, four take a truth as the object; and five, a person.
Walter Bauer, *A Greek-English Lexicon of the New Testament,*
trans. Wm. F. Arndt and F. Wilbur Gingrich (Chicago: University of Chicago Press, 1957), *in loco.*

32. *The Bible Today* (Cambridge: The University Press,
1948), p. 51.

33. This aspect of Bibliology was discussed by the older theologians under the head of "The Means of Grace." Because it was thus separated from the discussion of the inspiration and authority of the Bible and was generally tucked away in the remote sections of the last volume of their dogmatic systems, most contemporary theologians assume wrongly that the older dogmaticians had no doctrine of a present work of the Spirit in and through the written Word of Scripture. See Charles Hodge, *Systematic Theology*, 3 vols. (New York: Scribner, Armstrong & Co., 1873), III, pp. 466–84.

34. Harold de Wolf, Review of *Inspiration and Authority of the Bible* by Benjamin B. Warfield, *Journal of Bible and Religion*, XVII, No. 4 (October 1949), 273.

35. Professor Henry Joel Cadbury once remarked that the evidence for Jesus' view of the authority of the Old Testament was far more conclusive than that for Jesus' view of His own Messiahship.

36. See, for example, Hugh Mackintosh, *Is Christ Infallible and the Bible True?* (Edinburgh: T. & T. Clark, 1901); J. W. Wenham, *Our Lord's View of the Old Testament* (London: Tyndale Press, 1953); B. B. Warfield, *The Inspiration and Authority of the Bible* (Philadelphia: Presbyterian and Reformed Pub. Co., 1948); and R. Laird Harris, *Inspiration and Canonicity of the Bible* (Grand Rapids, Mich.: Zondervan, 1957).

37. *Time*, January 10, 1949, pp. 61–2.

38. Henry Nelson Wieman, "A Religious Naturalist Looks at Reinhold Niebuhr" in *Reinhold Niebuhr: His Religious, Social, and Political Thought*. Edited by Charles W. Kegley and Robert W. Bretall (New York: Macmillan, 1956), pp. 339–40.

39. *Das Christliche Verständnis der Offenbarung*, p. 19.

40. *The Wheaton Position on Inspiration*, Bible Department of Wheaton College. (Multilith material)

41. Brooke Foss Westcott and Fenton John Anthony Hort, *The New Testament in the Original Greek* (New York: Harper & Bros., 1882), p. 87. See also Frederick E. Kenyon, *Texts of the Greek Bible* (London: Duckworth, 1949), p. 252.

42. Cf. Emil Brunner, *Christian Doctrine of God*, p. 107;

and John Knox, *Jesus: Lord and Christ* (New York: Harper, 1958).

III. THE PERSON OF CHRIST

1. Mackintosh, H. R., *The Doctrine of the Person of Jesus Christ* (New York: Charles Scribner's Sons, 1921), pp. 1–121.

2. *The Lord of Glory* (Grand Rapids, Michigan: Zondervan Publishing House, reprint edition). In the following analysis I acknowledge a continuous indebtedness to both Warfield and Mackintosh.

3. Op. cit. pp. 302, 303.

4. Schleiermacher, Friedrich, *The Christian Faith* (Edinburgh: T. and T. Clark, 1928), p. 736.

5. Barth, Karl, *Dogmatics in Outline*. (New York: Philosophical Library, 1947), p. 84.

6. *Church Dogmatics*, I. 1, p. 474.

7. Brunner, Emil, *The Mediator* (Philadelphia: Westminster Press, 1947), pp. 78, 79.

8. Ibid. p. 240.

9. Ibid. p. 245.

10. Ibid. p. 248.

11. Ibid. pp. 275, 276.

12. Ibid. p. 319.

13. Ibid. 2, pp. 323–6.

14. *Church Dogmatics*, I. 2, p. 165, 167; as quoted in Weber, Otto. *Karl Barth's Church Dogmatics* (Philadelphia: Westminster Press, 1953), p. 46.

15. Knox, John, *On the Meaning of Christ* (New York: Charles Scribner's Sons, 1947), pp. 56–8.

16. Baillie, D. M., *God Was in Christ* (New York: Charles Scribner's Sons, 1948), p. 91f.

17. Ibid. pp. 130, 131.

18. Ibid. p. 145.

19. Tillich, Paul J., *Systematic Theology*, II (University of Chicago Press, 1957), p. 148.

20. That this is the case has, I think, been unanswerably argued

by Warfield in *The Inspiration and Authority of the Bible*. (Philadelphia: Presbyterian and Reformed Publishing Company, 1948: reprint), pp. 122–3, 138–44. Warfield shows that, like the claim to Christ's Deity, the appeal to absolute Scriptural authority by Jesus permeates all the sources and is therefore supported by the same weight as the claim to Deity itself.

21. Dodd, C. H., *The Authority of the Bible* (London: Nisbet and Company Ltd.), p. 233.

IV. REDEMPTION BY CHRIST

1. *Systematic Theology* (Philadelphia, Judson Press, 1907), p. 809.

2. Ibid. p. 829.

3. Ibid. p. 832.

V. CHRIST IN THE BELIEVER

1. Wade Crawford Barclay, *Early American Methodism*.

2. Harris Franklin Rall, "Sanctification" in *International Standard Bible Encyclopaedia*, p. 2684a.

3. Daniel Steele, "Sanctification: Wesleyan Doctrine" in *International Standard Bible Encyclopaedia*, p. 2686.

4. Charles G. Finney, *Sermons on Gospel Themes* (New York: Dodd, Mead & Co., 1876), pp. 373, 390.

VI. THE CHURCH OF GOD

1. Cremer: *Biblico-Theological Dictionary of the New Testament Greek*. On the appropriateness of this designation, see K. L. Schmidt's excellent treatment in Kittel's *Theologisches Worterbuch Zum Neuen Testament*. This most useful article on "The Church" is now available in an English translation, *Bible Key Words*, Adam and Charles Black, London.

2. Although *edhah* sometimes is translated into Greek by *ecclesia* it most frequently is rendered by *synagoge* (synagogue), the preferred term of Judaism.

3. T. F. Torrance, "The Israel of God," *Interpretation*, p. 306, July 1956.

4. Biblical references in this chapter are from both the American Revised Version and the King James Version.

5. Op. cit. p. 66.

6. L. Thornton, *The Common Life in the Body of Christ*, p. 144.

7. Markus Barth, "A Chapter on the Church—The Body of Christ," *Interpretation*, p. 145, April 1958.

8. Emil Brunner, *The Misunderstanding of the Church*, 1951, p. 48.

VII. CHRISTIAN ETHICS

1. *The Strategy and Tactics of World Communism* (Report of Sub-Committee #6, supplement #1, Committee on Foreign Affairs), p. 71.

2. Leander S. Keyser: *A Manual of Christian Ethics* (Burlington, Iowa: The Lutheran Literary Board, 1926), p. 10.

3. Carl F. H. Henry: *Christian Personal Ethics* (Grand Rapids, Mich.: Wm. B. Eerdmans Pub. Co., 1947), pp. 95, 96.

4. Ibid. p. 408.

VIII. THE HOPE OF THE WORLD

1. Emil Brunner, *Eternal Hope*, trans. Harold Knight (Philadelphia: The Westminster Press, 1954), p. 7.

2. *Service Hymnal*, 22, copyright by Hope Publishing Company.

3. Lewis Sperry Chafer, *Systematic Theology* (Dallas: Dallas Seminary Press, 1948), IV, 261.